PRAISE FOR *MALINCHE'S CONQUEST*, ALSO BY ANNA LANYON

'An imaginative, vivid reconstruction of a Mexican Indian woman who profoundly shaped New World history ... of much interest to historians and general readers alike.' —*Kirkus Reviews*

'Captivating' —*Der Spiegel*

'The story of Malinche's quest is mesmerising, and its telling to be relished, with the prose simple, spare, but lifting easily into poetry. Anyone who loves Mexico, old tales or fine prose should read this book.' —Inga Clendinnen, author of *The Aztecs*

'Provocative and engrossing' —*Booklist USA*

'This handsomely designed and beautifully written book is a loving rehabilitation of a woman maligned, brought in from the cold of a patriarchal history.' —*Sydney Morning Herald*

'Anna Lanyon's skilfully written and constructed, and beautifully presented book conveys the complexity while remaining unfailingly accessible and readable ... the resonant voice of an accomplished writer who has made the most of her subject.' —*The Weekend Australian*

'One of the pleasures of this book for me was the strength and richness with which it revivified the powerful old stories that I almost thought I'd forgotten ... the intensely personal tone of the writing only renders the analysis more complex and compelling.' —*Australian Book Review*

'The book offers readers a kind of insight into the way history can be re-created from the uncertainties of the past. Lanyon writes as if she is leading us on a journey of discovery.' —*The Canberra Times*

ANNA LANYON studied Spanish, Portuguese and History at La Trobe University in Melbourne. Anna is Honorary Visiting Research Fellow with that university's Institute of Latin American Studies and also with its School of Historical and European Studies. She is the award-winning author of *Malinche's Conquest* (1999) and co-producer of the documentary film *Malinche: The Noble Slave* (Saltillo Films, 2003). She lives in coastal Victoria and returns to Mexico whenever possible.

the new world of
MARTIN CORTES

ANNA LANYON

ALLEN&UNWIN

First published in 2003

This project has been assisted by the Commonwealth
Government through the Australia Council, its arts
funding and advisory board.

Allen & Unwin
83 Alexander Street
Crows Nest NSW 2065
Australia
Phone: (61 2) 8425 0100
Fax: (61 2) 9906 2218
Email: info@allenandunwin.com
Web: www.allenandunwin.com

National Library of Australia
Cataloguing-in-Publication entry:

Lanyon, Anna.
    The New World of Martin Cortes.

    ISBN 1 86508 728 9.

    1. Cortés, Martín, 1522–1569. 2. Spain—History—Charles I,
    1516–1556. 3. Mexico—History—Conquest, 1519–1540.
    4. Mexico—History—Spanish colony, 1540–1810. I. Title.

946.042

Consulting publisher: Jackie Yowell
Design by Ellie Exarchos
Set in 11.5/18pt Adobe Garamond by Asset Typesetting Pty Ltd
Printed in Australia by McPherson's Printing Group

10 9 8 7 6 5 4 3 2 1

For my family

Contents

List of illustrations

Preface

When Martín Cortés was born in 1522 the expression 'New World' was almost as young as he was. It had been coined only twenty-nine years earlier when a priest at the royal court of Spain inquired whether Columbus might accidentally have found a *novi orbus*, a new world, rather than India.

We know now that the priest was right — the landfall Columbus made in 1492, and the larger continent he skirted on his final voyage ten years later, were not India but parts of what would soon be called the 'Americas'. Yet the name 'las Indias' lingered on Spanish and Portuguese tongues. It occurs throughout the sixteenth-century references in this book, and persists to this day in the English terms 'West Indies' for the islands of the Caribbean, and 'Indian' for the Indigenous people of the Americas.

Martín Cortés was among the first children born in Mexico to an Amerindian mother and Spanish father in the aftermath of the Conquest. In that sense he was a true child of the New World. But when he arrived in Spain at the age of six, he entered another new world, for Europe at that time was caught up in the whirlwind of change we call the 'Renaissance', literally, the 'rebirth'. It was the threshold, the French historian, Fernand Braudel reminds us, of the world we now inhabit. This book is an attempt to follow Martín Cortés on his journeys back and forth between those colliding and evolving new worlds into which he was born, and in which he lived and died.

Readers who know Spanish will notice that in this text the surname 'Zavaleta' is written 'Cavaleta', as it was in 1568, and that some words commence with a double 'r' although this is something we no longer see in Spanish. 'Indias' — that linguistic remnant of Columbus's error — is almost always spelled 'Yndias'. 'Martín' is sometimes 'Martyn' — the way Martín Cortés himself spelled it — and 'Marina' is occasionally 'Maryna'. Similarly, the English chronicler, Robert Tomson, whose work appears in this text, spelled his surname without the 'h', rather than in the later form of 'Thomson'.

In his own time Hernán Cortés was called Fernando or Hernando, and sometimes Ferdinando. The name 'Hernán' is so familiar to modern readers, however, that I have used it in my text except where it occurs in sixteenth-century references. The Holy Roman Emperor in whose Spanish court Martín Cortés was raised was also a man of many names: Charles to the French and English, Karl to the Germans, Carolus in Latin, Carlos to the Spanish and Portuguese, and to the Indigenous people of the Americas. I have chosen Carlos for this book because it is his role as king of Spain with which the story of Martín Cortés is mostly, although not exclusively, concerned. As for my own English spelling, years of reading and writing Spanish have given me a love for the uncluttered and original Latin forms like *labor, color* and *honor,* and for the older suffix *–ize* in words like *realize* and *organize.*

Preface

One last comment on language: the Spanish word *mestizo* is often translated into English as 'half-caste' or 'half-breed', yet at a deep semantic level *mestizo* is very different from those terms. It does not share their connotations of something halved, or diminished, or lessened. *Mestizo* is derived from Latin *miscere*, to mix, or fuse or blend, and that is all it means: mixed. In Mexico today, where the majority of people are descended from both Amerindian and Spanish ancestors, *mestizo* is not an offensive word, but a symbol of the 'epic marriage', as the writer Richard Rodriguez calls the Spanish Conquest, out of which Martín Cortés and modern Mexico were born.

I wish to make clear that any blunders, infelicities or misinterpretations in this book are entirely my doing and not the fault of those who were kind enough to help me along the way. I am deeply grateful to the Literature Board of the Australia Council for giving me a Developing Writers Grant for this book and with it, time to think, to develop ideas, to research and write. Dr Barry Carr, Director of La Trobe University's Institute of Latin American Studies, and Professor Tim Murray of that university's School of Historical and European Studies, supported me with Honorary Visiting Research Fellowships. They helped me more than they know, both through their encouragement, and the practical assistance those fellowships offered me.

People in many places gave me companionship, support, and advice: Isabel Aguirre, Robyn Annear, Edith Barry, José Borghino, Barbie Burton, Ezequial Castillo Rojas, Carmen

Celestino, Julian Clorbuth, Gloria and Kevin Council, Sabine Dörlemann, Christian Dittüs, Leo Donnelly, Ariadna Flores Aguilar, Linden Gillbank, Carlos Gómez Figueroa, Pablo Gómez de Orozco, Elena Gonzalez Bouret, Vittoria Grossi, Dr Julia Frederick, Robert Hamilton, Irmgard Heidler, Anne Henderson, Tess Howells, Monica Iseli, Dr Miguel Izusqui, Lesley Jackson, Professor Henry Kamen, Laura Kuhlmann Zamora, Elaine Lindsay, Sally Lowe, Andreas Lueg, Jackie Maling, Dr Luis Montiel, Cristal Ortiz, Tony Parsons, Alicia Rosas Castillo, Jacob Rothfield, Dr Rose Rothfield, Steve Rothfield, Rafael Santa Anna Flores, Dr Christina Slade, Pam Stringer, Walter Struve, Gonzalo Vega Gonzalez, Anne Whitehead and Peter Woodruff.

Jorge Eduardo Ortiz Moore gave me a home in Mexico City. He and Dr Ricardo Melgar in Cuernavaca did much to help me in the final stages of this book. Pilar Melero Avitía, Sara Luz Flores and Malena Gurrola became my dear *companeras*. I thank all of them from the depths of my heart. Dr Victoria Vincent shared with me her deep knowledge of the Avila-Cortés conspiracy trials of 1566–68, while her husband, Professor Rob Ewart, used his technical wizardry to get her dissertation to me across the Pacific in rapid time. I want to thank Trina Paevere for reminding me about the plaque in the Plaza de Las Tres Culturas which I had seen and then, somehow, forgotten. I count it as a small miracle that we met and talked together just before this book was completed.

Preface

My daughters, Lucie and Anna, were willing research assistants on many occasions. Amy Reid Lescoe and Alejandro Valdés Rochín became my friends during the writing of this book. I treasure their help, and our collaboration, more than I can say. My publisher, and friend, Jackie Yowell, has given many hours to the shaping of this text, and sustained me far beyond the call of duty, as she did throughout the writing of my first book. I am deeply grateful to Christa Munns, Senior Editor at Allen & Unwin, for remaining patient, calm and brave throughout, and for guiding me to another safe landing. I thank Colette Vella who read the page proofs with sensitivity, and offered much good and timely advice. I am overwhelmed by the artistry of designer Ellie Exarchos who has evoked the face of Martín Cortés with such poignant beauty.

My family, Vincent and Norma, Lucie and Anna, David and Patrick, Jessie and Harry, have given me encouragement, support and inspiration throughout this long journey, and I dedicate this book to them.

Anna Lanyon
Cape Duchesne, June 2003

✠ Old World Spain ✠

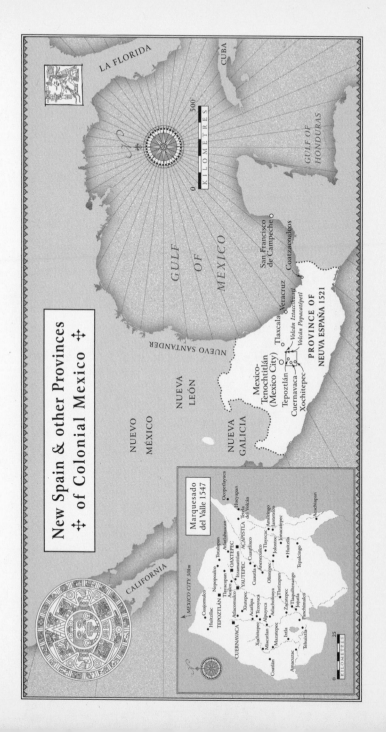

New Spain & other Provinces
‡ of Colonial Mexico ‡

LA FLORIDA

CUBA

GULF OF
MEXICO

GULF OF
HONDURAS

0   500   KILOMETRES

NUEVO SANTANDER

San Francisco
de Campeche

Coatzacoalcos

Tlaxcala ○ Veracruz
Mexico-
Tenochtitlán
(Mexico City)   Volcán Iztaccíhuatl
Tepoztlán ○   Volcán Popocatépetl
Cuernavaca ○
Xochitepec ○   PROVINCE OF
NEUVA ESPAÑA 1521

NUEVO
MÉXICO

NUEVA
LEÓN

NUEVA
GALICIA

CALIFORNIA

Marquesado
del Valle 1547

MEXICO CITY 56km →

Ocopellayuca

Cuajomulco   Nepopoalco
Huitzilac   Tlayacapan   Totolapan
TEPOZTLÁN   Atlatlauhcan
Atlacomulco   Tlalnepantla   Hueyapan
Tlacotepec   OAXTEPEC   Tetela
Xiutepec   Tlaltizapan   del Volcán
CUERNAVACA   YAUTEPEC   ACAPISTA
Acatlipa   Cuautla   Cuauhtlixco
Temoac
Tepoztlán ○ Xochitepec Tecoyoca   Amenequilco
Mixcatlan   Alpuyeca   Olintepec   Tlayaca   Anilzingo
Mazatepec   Atlacholoaya   Yolotoco   Jonacatepec
Zacatepec   Tlaltizapan   Jantetelco
Coatlan   Istla   Tepalcingo   Huitzila
Amacuzac   Tehuixtla   Pinchimalco
Axochiapan

0   25   KILOMETRES

'So we must then discover the path they followed in the journeying from the Old World into the New ... for it has to be that they came, not sailing upon the ocean, but walking upon the earth.'

JOSÉ DE ACOSTA,
Historia Natural y Moral de las Indias, 1590

Conquistador's Son

Thou Art an Ocelot

In Mexico City once, in the square they call the Plaza de Las Tres Culturas, I came upon a plaque that overwhelmed me with its sadness, and its hope.

The plaque recalled the day in August 1521 when the city, then an Aztec metropolis, finally surrendered to its Spanish conquerors after months of siege and battle. 'It was neither a triumph nor a defeat,' it said. 'It was the painful birth, *el doloroso nacimiento*, of the mixed race of people, *del pueblo mestizo*, who are the Mexico of today.'

It was my first visit to Mexico, and my first experience of the pride and anguish with which Mexicans regard the terrible events that brought them into being. I didn't realize then that soon after the surrender referred to in the plaque, not far across the city from where I stood that cold January morning, a child had been born who, more than any of the numerous children born to Amerindian mothers and Spanish fathers in the aftermath of the Conquest, could be said to symbolize that agonizing genesis of the new Mexico.

The child's name was Martín Cortés. His father was Hernán Cortés, the Spanish conquistador to whom the Aztec city surrendered in August 1521. His mother was the young Amerindian woman called Marina or Malintzin or Malinche, depending on which language we use to name her, who had served Cortés as guide and interpreter throughout the years of the Conquest.

As the child of such parents, born at such a catastrophic moment in history, how could Martín Cortés not be regarded as the first 'Mexican', the first *mestizo* in a land of mestizos?

He was born in an Aztec palace his father had commandeered on the southern outskirts of the fallen city, in what is now the wealthy suburb of Coyoacán. The palace was a household of women. His mother, Malinche, was there; so were three of the Aztec emperor's daughters who had been captured during the final battle for Tenochtitlán. The Spanish wife of Hernán Cortés was also resident, for now that the fighting was over she had come to join her husband. But her time in his household proved unhappy and by November she was dead.

Few Spanish women were present in the fallen city at that time, so Malinche must have been assisted during childbirth by an Aztec woman who had survived the long siege the previous year. No-one knows this now-forgotten midwife's name, but as she cut Martín's umbilical cord she would have invoked the traditional blessing for a male infant, calling him her precious son, her youngest one, telling him he was an eagle, an ocelot. 'Thy home is not here,' she would have murmured to him, 'for war is thy destiny, war is thy mission … Perhaps thou shalt receive the gift … perhaps thou shalt prove worthy of death by the obsidian knife.'

Death in war, death by the obsidian knife: it was the most honorable fate such a woman could envisage for a male child in her society. But this boy was a child of two worlds. Whatever prayers his Aztec nurse may have uttered in her own Náhuatl language, whatever secret name his mother might have given him in the hours following his birth, his father's world was also waiting to claim him. Therefore some time later that day or night one of the four European priests in Mexico at that time entered the room to perform the ritual of Christian baptism.

Did Cortés cradle his son in his arms during the ceremony, or hand him to the godfather he must have appointed for him? These details about the earliest moments of Martín's life were not recorded. We know only that the officiating priest blessed the child in Latin in the name of the Father, the Son and the Holy Spirit and, while pouring holy water over his small head, baptized him with the name his father had chosen for him: 'Martín' in memory of the Roman god of war; 'Martín' in memory of the soldier-saint, Martín de Tours; 'Martín' in honor of Hernán Cortés's own beloved father in Spain. It was the most precious name he could imagine for his first-born son.

I think of him as Malinche's child, but I know now he was probably taken from her when he was very young.

In 1942, in a small biography entitled *Doña Marina, La Dama de la Conquista*, which was the name the Spaniards gave Malinche, a descendant of Martín Cortés said that when Martín was around two years old his father took him from his mother and placed him in the care of one of his kinsmen, a man called Juan Altamirano. The descendant who related this story was the distinguished Mexican historian, Federico

Gómez de Orozco. He offered no evidence for his forlorn assertion, so perhaps it had been handed down through his family. But wherever he had heard it, it makes sense when we consider what happened to Martín's mother in 1524, when Martín was two.

In October that year Hernán Cortés set out from Mexico-Tenochtitlán, as the city was now called, for the Gulf of Honduras, fourteen hundred kilometres away in the south. He went in order to suppress a rebellion by mutinous Spaniards who had settled on the Gulf and rebelled against his authority, and he took Malinche with him as his guide and interpreter. It was a role she knew well; she had served him in this way almost from the moment she was given to him five years earlier by the Mayans. But the journey to Honduras was to be her last expedition with him and it marked the end, in public at least, of their intimate liaison. In late October, a few weeks after they left Mexico-Tenochtitlán, she was married to another Spaniard on the expedition, a man called Juan Xaramillo.

It was a momentous journey for Malinche. Two months after she married Xaramillo their expedition reached the coast, near the present-day city of Coatzacoalcos, and there Malinche came face to face for the first time in many years

MALINCHE INTERPRETING FOR HERNÁN CORTÉS, C. 1550
Lienzo de Tlaxcala

with her mother and her half-brother. A young conquistador called Bernal Diaz del Castillo was among those who witnessed their tearful reunion. He said that some months earlier Malinche had told him that when she was a child her mother had sold her into slavery, in order to ensure this half-brother's ascendancy in the family. He watched as Malinche forgave her weeping mother for what she had done so long ago, and he likened what he saw to the moment in the Book of Genesis when Joseph is reunited with the brothers who had sold him into slavery in Egypt.

It seemed to Bernal Diaz del Castillo that in Coatzacoalcos Malinche had acted with true Christian forgiveness, and perhaps she did, for there is no reason to suspect she was not a sincere convert to Christianity. But I wonder now whether her compassion toward her mother was also influenced by a more elemental kind of insight, one that Diaz del Castillo did not recognize: by the pain of knowing how it felt to relinquish a child.

After Coatzacoalcos the expedition became a two-year nightmare as Cortés entered the difficult Mayan realms of the south for the first time. He watched helplessly as hundreds of his previously invincible companions died of malnutrition or tropical diseases, or drowned in swollen rivers and marshes along the way, and Bernal Diaz del Castillo noticed that he took to drinking, which was something he had never done in the past.

Malinche survived. With her usual fortitude she walked from what is now Mexico City to the Gulf of Honduras. She was pregnant for much of the journey, and during a hurricane on the return voyage in 1526 she gave birth to a daughter. But it is unthinkable that her small son could have come through such an ordeal, even with the protection of such a mother. By the age of two he would have been old enough to be weaned, old enough, therefore, to be given into the care of someone else, rather than dragged to an early death in Honduras.

Four centuries later, in his book about Malinche, Federico Gómez de Orozco said that after she went to Honduras her son was 'always in the house of Juan Altamirano, *siempre estaba en la casa de Juan Altamirano.*' The precise circumstances of their separation have never come to light, however. We do not know whether she agreed to re-linquish Martín, or fought to keep him. She had every reason to fear the journey to Honduras, and may well have been persuaded that it was safer for him to be given to Juan Altamirano, in case she did not return. But we should not assume she had any say in his destiny, for she was a young and stateless woman and in no position to argue with a man like Hernán Cortés in whatever he decided for their child, or to provide for Martín without his support.

How did Malinche endure her loss? The letter Cortés wrote later to his emperor, Carlos V, to describe the journey to Honduras, suggests she carried out her duties as interpreter with her usual competence and courage. But she must have yearned in secret for her child the way women through the ages have always yearned for their lost children; the way Indigenous Australian women still grieve for the mixed-race children taken from them by white authorities throughout the twentieth century. And what of Martín Cortés? Did he weep as he was taken from his mother's arms? He must have done, although this too is something we should not presume, for some cultures, Amerindian cultures among them, discourage tears and encourage stoicism, even in small children.

Few of us have memories of our earliest years and, as I followed his trail through life, I found no overt expressions of loss and longing among his papers, and nothing to suggest that as an adult he remembered anything of his mother. But absence of conscious memory does not mean that in the years that followed their separation he did not yearn for her warmth, her smell, for the Náhuatl or Mayan words she must have murmured to him from the day he was born.

It was September 1526 by the time Malinche returned to Mexico-Tenochtitlán with her new Spanish husband and her infant daughter. For the next three years she lived in an elegant house three blocks north of the city's central plaza while her son, who was now four years old, apparently remained in the Altamirano house, three blocks south of the plaza. The physical distance between them was slight therefore, so slight that it is possible they glimpsed each other from time to time in the great square that lay between them.

Malinche would have known her child, even after two years separation, for few mestizo boys and girls lived the privileged life he lived, or were seen, as he was, in the care of a rich and well-known Spaniard like Juan Altamirano. But Martín may not have recognized her, for one of her servants said later that she dressed always in the costume of an Indian, *en el habito de yndia*, and never adopted Spanish clothes. To her son she may have looked like any other Amerindian woman in the streets of Mexico-Tenochtitlán. In any case, this mother and child had little time for a reunion because in March 1528, when he was almost six, Martín left for his new life in Spain and, by the time he returned to Mexico in 1562, Malinche had been dead for thirty years.

'All humans suffer exile from the paradise of the mother, in fact or in later wistful imaginings,' says Inga Clendinnen in *Aztecs*, her study of Aztec life before the coming of the

Spaniards. So it seems it was for Martín Cortés, exiled from his mother, and his land of birth, at an early age.

He may have come quietly into the world of Mexico-Tenochtitlán, but his departure for Spain six years later was more conspicuous. He went as a member of his father's entourage, and after twenty-three years in the Americas, Hernán Cortés took care to ensure his return would be noticed. He gathered together a party of Aztec musicians and acrobats, conjurers, dwarfs and albinos and, like a sixteenth-century Noah, he collected ocelots and jaguars, armadillos, opossums, monkeys of various kinds, hummingbirds and quetzals, with their magnificent turquoise tail-feathers.

He also took with him three of the Aztec emperor's sons whom he intended to present at the royal court of Spain. One of them was known as Martín Cortés Nezahualzolotl, because Cortés had honored him as well with his father's name; so two passengers called Martín Cortés set sail for Spain that March of 1528 — one an Aztec prince, the other a small mestizo boy.

There is something about that name — something about the way it resounds like an echo through this story. Four years later Cortés would give it to another of his children, this time to a son born to him by the Spanish noblewoman to whom he was already betrothed. In doing so he left us the promise of a family story as absurd as Shakespeare's tale of the twins called Antipholus, as tragic as the saga of Ishmael and his half-brother, Isaac.

But in March 1528, when Malinche's child sailed for Europe, he was still his father's only son. He had three half-sisters, one of whom was the grand-daughter of the Aztec emperor, but the half-brother who would share his name was not yet born, and the great ordeal that awaited Martín Cortés when he returned to Mexico lay far into the future.

Spain

I always wondered how closely and how far I could trace Martín Cortés, this child of the Conquest. I think of him as Malinche's child, but it was his father who shaped his life, and his father's path in life I had to follow in order to understand the boy's early years in Spain.

Martín Cortés had lived on two continents, and in two worlds, with an ocean in between, so following him would not be a simple linear journey. I sensed that I would sometimes cross his path without realizing until it was too late to turn back. But I also knew that even if he left only a faint trail through the European years of his life, once he returned to Mexico and the most dangerous moments of his life, he would turn and I would see him far more clearly.

I took copies of Cortés's letters with me to Spain. Not the famous five letters, the *Cartas de Relación* he had written to Carlos V as he sought to impress him with his exploits in Mexico and Honduras, but the more candid letters he wrote to his father in the aftermath of the Conquest.

I felt certain Cortés must have told his father about his child. He had no reason to conceal Martín's existence, for recognition of illegitimate children was common among aristocrats and men of the lesser nobility, like Cortés. But I never found such a reference, and if a letter ever existed it may have gone missing during one of the long trans-Atlantic voyages between Mexico and Spain, or have been misplaced in some forgotten archive.

I found another letter Cortés had written to his father not long before he left Mexico, however, and thought I saw in it something of the tenderness he might have used in describing his son. 'Señor,' he began, 'here in my house we have raised a tiger since it was very small. It has grown into the most beautiful animal one could ever see because, apart from being beautiful, it is very tame and walks freely through the house and eats whatever it is given from the table. I believe it could travel quite safely in the ship,' he continued, 'and so I ask your Honor that it be given to His

Majesty, for in truth it is a gift worth giving.' He signed the letter simply and respectfully *vuestro hijo*, your son.

But his father never read that description of the little animal that must in reality have been an ocelot or jaguar, for by the time the letter made its way across the Atlantic he was dead. He had died before his son, Cortés, could show him the 'tiger' he had found in Mexico, and the small mestizo grandson he had named after him.

Even in the cooler months of spring the ancient Spanish seaport of Palos de la Frontera lies shimmering in heat. It was once a busy threshold to the Americas, but the shipbuilders and chandlers, the navigators and pilots are gone now. The Odiel river remains, however, flowing silently by as it did when it carried Columbus out into the Atlantic, past the west coast of Africa and on toward the unknown western lands he mistook for India.

The ship in which the child Martín Cortés left Mexico with his father sailed into the harbor of Palos de la Frontera in May 1528. No reporters, no cameras or microphones were there to record his impressions as he took his first steps on Spanish soil, and none of the contemporary historians who described his father's disembarkation at Palos was actually there in person. So accounts of his arrival have come down to us in fragments rather than through one clear reliable testimony.

People working on the wharves at Palos that day must have paused to marvel at the strange birds and animals, the Aztec acrobats and conjurers and nobles that Cortés had brought with him from the far side of the Atlantic. Amid such wonders they probably did not notice a small and silent child who walked beside his father, or in the care of a servant. Martín Cortés was the son of an Amerindian woman, but he had been raised among Spaniards and was, to all intents and purposes, a Spanish boy dressed, we must presume, like any other son of a wealthy father — in a velvet cap and doublet, a cape, long stockings and ribboned shoes.

The province of Andalucía in which he found himself had known the mixing of races for longer and to a greater extent that any other province or principality in Western Europe. When Hernán Cortés was Martín's age it had still been an Islamic kingdom called Al Andaluz, where Muslims wrote Arabic in Roman script, where Jews wrote Hebrew in Arabic script, and where Christian knights fought in the service of Muslim princes. In such a place a child's almond eyes, the copper patina of his skin, and the straight and silken blackness of his hair might not have aroused much curiosity.

But even if the people of Palos did not notice Martín Cortés, he must have noticed them. In Mexico-Tenochtitlán, where he was born, Spaniards were still few and the faces in the streets belonged to the vanquished Aztecs. In Palos in 1528 the only Amerindian faces were those of the passengers who had crossed from the far side of the Atlantic with him, although, had he looked into a mirror, he might have seen something of their features reflected in his own.

He would have seen Christian women in broad, far-thingale skirts, veiled Muslim women in silken slippers and voluminous pantaloons, and men, women and children of both faiths begging ransoms for the rescue of their loved ones enslaved in North Africa. The Jews were gone, however; most had been sent into exile almost forty years earlier, and the few who remained took care to conceal their identity beneath a Christian exterior.

In Spain that spring I learned that despite the great conquest Hernán Cortés had accomplished in what is now Mexico, when he sailed into the harbor at Palos de la Frontera in

May 1528 he was still relatively unknown. The five long letters he had written to his king and emperor between 1519 and 1526 had been published to acclaim in Augsburg and Milan, but in Spain, where recognition meant everything to him, their publication had been suppressed. This prohibition seems perplexing now, given the mighty empire we know would evolve out of his endeavors, but Spain in 1528 was deeply suspicious of Hernán Cortés.

It was still just a fledgling confederacy of Christian provinces. Its king, the king to whom Cortés had written those famous letters, was not a Spaniard but a prince from Ghent in present-day Belgium who spoke little Spanish and had yet to win his people's loyalty. He had only recently survived a violent rebellion against his rule, and his advisers, anxious for him and for their emergent nation, distrusted this maverick adventurer called Hernán Cortés who had undertaken the invasion of an unknown world without royal permission, and seemed intent on gathering power to himself on the other side of the Atlantic.

Cortés knew about the suspicion emanating out of the royal court toward him. He had returned to Mexico-Tenochtitlán from Honduras to find that the Crown's officials had arrived in his absence and confiscated the lands he had claimed for himself after the Conquest. They had also tortured and executed the cousin he had left behind as his representative.'I am in purgatory,' he told his father in a letter of September 1526. He said he could not write about what had happened, because of the pain it caused him. He would rather be rich in fame and memory, he added, than in worldly goods.

In response his father warned him that the emperor's advisers intended bringing him to Spain in chains for disciplinary proceedings, for he was technically a rebel against the Crown. So it was in anticipation of that threat that Cortés departed Mexico in March 1528. It is curious to think he did not return to his homeland voluntarily or in triumph, because from this distance in time it can appear that way. But the truth is that he returned to Spain to present his case before the emperor and seek forgiveness for his transgressions.

In the quiet winding streets of Palos I asked some Moroccan children if they could tell me how to find the monastery of Santa Maria de La Rábida. They pointed down the estuary and assured me it was not far. It took me little time to walk there beneath palm trees whose fronds moved slowly in the breeze from the Atlantic. Inside the monastery I noticed that its intricately patterned cloister walls reflected Islam's love of decorative harmony, while the refectory had been painted pure white in Franciscan austerity. In the chapel beyond the patio, candles burned before a modest altar, while high above me on the wall Saint Francis of Assisi knelt in the scarlet, black and gold light of a single stained-glass window.

During the age of exploration, navigators, explorers and conquistadors had come to Santa Maria de La Rábida to pray before setting out on their journeys. When and if they returned they made their way back to the monastery to give thanks. In 1490 Columbus had brought his small, motherless son to the monastery and asked the Franciscans to take care of him while he went in search of royal backing for his voyage to India. Thirty-eight years later Martín Cortés, who was also a motherless child, arrived with his father at Santa Maria de La Rábida.

They rested for some weeks in one of its small white rooms, and there is a famous story that while they were there Hernán Cortés had a chance meeting with his kinsman, Francisco Pizarro, who was then setting out on his own adventure in the Americas. It is a good story, but an apocryphal one, for although Pizarro did return to Spain in 1528, and the two men may have met at some point, it could not have been at La Rábida, for in May that year Pizarro was probing the northern seaboard of the land he called 'Biru' in preparation for his conquest of the Incas four years later.

From the monastery doors I looked out toward the palm trees above the estuary. I stood in shadow but the warmth of the spring sun outside suggested the furnace this place would become in July and August. In my hand I held a thousand-peseta note. Hernán Cortés looked out at me from one side, his cousin, Francisco Pizarro, from the other. The famous scar below Cortés's lip — the one the conquistador-chronicler, Bernal Diaz del Castillo, said he had received in a knife fight over a woman — had been erased. His face was benignly handsome, and his costume belonged to the late sixteenth century rather than his own time. Only two portraits of Cortés had been drawn from life, and this was not one of them.

I remembered something else Bernal Diaz del Castillo had said in his famous memoir of the Conquest. He recalled that in April 1519, as they sailed along the unknown coast of what is now Mexico, gazing out toward the massive snowcapped peak of Citlaltepetl, one of their comrades-in-arms had approached Cortés and recited some verses from a popular ballad they all knew. It told the story of a nobleman whose enemies had turned the king against him and forced him into exile. But finally, after years away, he returned and was restored to his rightful place in his king's affections.

Diaz del Castillo said that Cortés had understood what his friend was implying as he recited those verses: that although the adventure on which he had embarked was not sanctioned by the Spanish Crown, although in setting sail for the American mainland Cortés had disobeyed the governor of Cuba, he would be forgiven in the end, and rewarded for his pains.

Now, nine years later, Cortés had come home to seek that redemption. He was certain that if he impressed the emperor, Carlos V, with the magnificence of his achievement and the depth of his loyalty, he would be forgiven. He might even find a place at the royal court for his son. But first he had to pay his respects to his mother, and to his father's memory, in the small village in the province of Extremadura, where he had been born.

In Mexico the old Amerindian placenames still command the ancient landscape. In Spain the topography is ruled by Rome and Islam.

The Romans gave the province of Extremadura its name: they called it Extrema Durii to denote its remote position beyond the Duero river. Eventually the region was overrun by the Berbers of North Africa, who stayed for eight centuries until Christian Spain arose around the middle of the fifteenth century to reclaim Extremadura.

It was from this much-conquered province that the first conquistadors set out for the Americas — Cortés, Pizarro, Soto, Alvarado, Balboa, Almagro — all those names that have resonated down through the centuries. To be an Extremeño, a man from Extremadura, was sufficient to ensure inclusion in the great early expeditions of Spanish conquest when men defined themselves by their kinship, their province and their faith, when the idea of nationality had barely begun to form in their minds. The Extremeños were young — Cortés had been nineteen when he left for Cuba; Pizarro and Almagro were even younger. They were physically strong, and driven by their poverty and a hunger for whatever fortune might offer them.

They had grown up among the Roman ruins of their province, and seemed always deeply conscious of its influence. Bernal Diaz del Castillo recalled that Cortés liked to invoke the deeds of Julius Caesar as he urged his frequently mutinous men to remain steadfast in the face of the uncertainties and the peril they faced every day in Mexico. His grand allusions seemed to work. 'Cortés went on to develop some comparisons with the heroic deeds of the Romans,' Diaz del Castillo said after one rebellious incident, 'and we all answered to a man that we would obey his orders, and that the die was cast for good fortune, as Caesar said at the Rubicon.'

When the men from Extremadura reached the far side of the Atlantic they scattered the old Roman names of their province across the face of the Americas, so that a Mayan town in southern Mexico received the name Merida in memory of the emperor Augustus, Augusta Emerita, while other towns and cities were named Medellin for a Roman Consul called Metelus who lived seventy years before Christ. The original Medellin, in eastern Extremadura, is the place where Hernán Cortés was born. It is a small and pretty village beside the serene waters of the Guadiana river, close to Portugal, and very far removed in its geography and its milieu from the dangerous streets of its Colombian namesake.

I went by train to Medellin, and I travelled alone and unencumbered. But the procession in which six-year-old Martín

Cortés journeyed north with his father from Palos — along dusty roads haunted by vagabonds and former galley slaves — must have moved with unbearable slowness through the early summer of 1528. The mountains of western Andalucia are high and their valleys deep. The Sierra de Aracena extends west toward Portugal, the dark hills and cork forests of the Sierra Morena stretch east toward Córdoba, and it is not until you clear the mountains and emerge into the open plains of Extremadura that it is possible to move more swiftly.

In the plaza at Medellin I found the empty space where the Cortés family's house had once stood. A plaque told me it had been damaged when Napoleon's forces swept through Extremadura in 1804 and demolished by order of the municipal authorities a century later, for by then the ruined building was considered dangerous.

But I had only to raise my eyes above the tiled rooftops to see what Cortés saw every day when he was a child growing up in Medellin: a huge and formidable castle keeping watch over the village, and the roads beyond leading east to Córdoba and west to Portugal. His son, Malinche's child, would have seen it too, in 1528, and wondered at its immensity, for the temples and pyramids of the Aztec capital were in ruins by the time he was born.

I climbed the path toward the castle and found a botanical symbol of his homeland — a large cactus of the kind that attracts hummingbirds and hawk-moths — growing against its upper walls. From the castle walls I could see for miles around. I could see the great white storks nesting on the village rooftops and the Guadiana river flowing silently beneath the ancient stone bridge. Below me stood the church of San Martín, where Hernán Cortés was baptized, and the church of Santiago, where his father had been buried. In the distance I saw the river plains where Cortés's mother had owned some beehives, a vineyard and a mill, from which she earned a small income.

In the capricious record we call history some names survive down through the centuries while others are lost forever. I did not know the name of Martín Cortés's midwife, but I knew who his father's wet-nurse was, and even where she came from. She was a woman called Maria de Esteban from the nearby village of Oliva, and she had prayed to Saint Peter for the infant Hernán Cortés because he seemed so weak and sickly. I knew these tiny details because Cortés had told them to his chaplain and biographer, Francisco López de Gómara, and he in turn had recorded them for posterity.

Childhood ended early in sixteenth-century Europe. As

a small boy Hernán Cortés is believed to have left home with his father, and together they journeyed to the great houses of the province as the elder Martín Cortés sought a position as a pageboy for his son. He was not successful, so they returned to the village by the river and there Cortés remained until the age of fourteen, when he left for Salamanca, to study law.

López de Gómara said Cortés's mother was a pious and frugal woman called Catalina Pizarro Altamirano. She was still in Medellin when Cortés returned there with his son in 1528. Like her husband, the first Martín Cortés, she belonged to the lesser nobility, and was an 'Old Christian', which is to say she was not descended from Sephardic Jews or Muslims, a crucial distinction in sixteenth-century Spain.

Her opinion of her first grand-child, the younger Martín Cortés, is not recorded, but the boy's racial inheritance probably did not trouble her, as it might have done if his mother had been a Jewish or a Moorish woman. The Conquest of Mexico was so recent, and its people so unknown in Spain, that they were spared such ancient prejudices.

López de Gómara described her husband, the first Martín Cortés, as honest and devout like his wife, and a charitable man. These were virtues any respectable Spaniard of that time would wish to claim. But López de Gómara did record one startling fact about the elder Martín Cortés. He said that as a young man he had fought for a patrician kinsman of his called Alonso de Monroy against the forces of Queen Isabella and King Ferdinand as they struggled to control their unruly Christian nobles.

Monroy had lost his battle in the end. He was banished from Spain forever while, for reasons that have never been clear, Martín Cortés was pardoned for his role in the affair and escaped punishment. What I noticed in this story was its suggestion that the thread of rebellion that would run through the Cortés family, and ensnare Malinche's child when he returned to Mexico, had begun with his grandfather, fighting against the Spanish Crown on the warring plains of fifteenth-century Extremadura.

In June 1528 Hernán Cortés left Medellin for the third time. He took his son, Martín, his Aztec nobles and acrobats and conjurers, and went in search of his emperor. But finding him was not easy. Carlos V was in every way a Renaissance prince, not a sedentary monarch of the kind we have grown accustomed to in recent centuries. Carlos was physically strong, disciplined and skilled in warfare. He already embodied many of the ideals contained in Machiavelli's not-yet-published work, *Il Principe*, The Prince. He galloped constantly across the plains and mountains of his new Spanish realm, learning how steep its mountains were, where its plains lay, the nature of its rivers and marshes, just as Machiavelli would recommend a prince must do. Like his grandparents, Isabella and Ferdinand, Carlos had no permanent capital. Instead he held court in palaces and castles borrowed from Spanish nobles throughout the country.

Perhaps that is why there is so much confusion about where Cortés finally caught up with him. López de Gómara thought it was in Toledo, but he was still a child of seven at the time and did not witness their meeting. Others have suggested Monzón or Valladolid, even Madrid, perhaps mistakenly assuming that the present Spanish capital was then the seat of government. Cortés himself mentions Barcelona in a letter he wrote to Carlos V two years later, after he had returned to Mexico: 'After I kissed Your Majesty's hands in Barcelona,' he said, 'and gave you an account of the things that had happened in New Spain', which was the new name the Spaniards had recently given to what is now Mexico. So perhaps it was in the Catalan capital that he came face to face at last with his emperor. Wherever their meeting took place, it was autumn, and López de Gómara said that by then the royal court had heard news of the fabulous entourage Cortés had brought with him from the Americas, 'and everyone longed to see him'.

Carlos V was twenty-eight, the same age as his century. I have heard him called 'the first and last great emperor of Europe' and even 'the first European'. It is a fitting description for such a man. He had been Count of Flanders, Duke of Burgundy and Milan, King of Spain and Naples since childhood. When Cortés knelt before him he was preparing to leave for Bologna and his coronation as Holy Roman Emperor. The portraits Dürer, Titian, Vermeyan and Leoni made of Carlos V throughout his life, in gold, in wood and ivory, reveal the same expressive face, the same large, inquiring eyes, and always, above his luxurious robes and fur collars, the famous angular Habsburg jaw.

He was devoted all his life to music, as well as to art and war and imperial politics. He loved the ravishing polyphony of the Flemish singers and musicians of his homeland, and they accompanied him wherever he went, even into battle. It is possible they were singing as Cortés and his delegation entered Carlos V's presence in the autumn of 1528. But whether they entered to silence, or to the glorious cadences of the Flemish singers with their intricate melodic lines, López de Gómara says that Carlos V received his errant conquistador, who was fifteen years his senior, with great affection. Bernal Diaz del Castillo went a little further in his own account of the meeting. He said the emperor took Cortés's hands, raised him from his knees and led him to a seat of honor beside him.

As always with Diaz del Castillo, we hear the resonance of an Old Testament story, or an echo of one of the romances of chivalry he loved to read, and sense that allegory may be at work in his telling of things. But it is true that despite those years of tension and suspicion, the emperor seems to have forgiven Cortés his transgressions when he came before him in 1528. He even created a new aristocratic title for him — 'the Marqués del Valle de Oaxaca' — a title abbreviated ever after to the 'Marqués del Valle' since 'Oaxaca', a Zapotec word from southern Mexico, was as daunting to sixteenth-century Spaniards as it is to English speakers now.

It was an age of restless journeying, not only for conquistadors, their children and their captives, but also for artists. While Cortés and his son, Martín, were making their way north

HERNÁN CORTÉS BY CHRISTOPH WEIDITZ, 1529

Germanisches National Museum, Nuremberg

through Extremadura, a young German engraver called
Christoph Weiditz had been traveling south to Spain from
Augsburg to present himself to Carlos V and ask for his
patronage. He was at court when Cortés arrived in autumn
1528, and early the following year he prepared sketches of
Cortés's retinue for his costume book, the *Trachtenbuch*.

Weiditz drew an Aztec noble in a long feathered cloak, another with a lorikeet perched on his shoulder, two acrobats tossing and balancing large wooden rollers on their feet, and a pair of lithe athletes playing a game with a kind of ball never before seen in Europe. López de Gómara said the ball was 'made of the gum of the *ulli*, a tree of the hot country. When slashed,' he continued in this early account of rubber, '[it] oozes thick white drops that soon harden … they are rolled into balls which … bounce and jump very well, better than our inflated ones.'

In plate number IV of his *Trachtenbuch*, Weiditz drew Cortés in a doublet with voluminous sleeves and a fine, dark, pleated *sayo*, or jerkin, probably of black velvet: black for constancy, and to show that he was a serious and loyal servant of his king. He leaned slightly to the right, his sword at his side, his right hand on his hip, while in his left he held the coat of arms with which Carlos V had just presented him.

Bernal Diaz del Castillo described him later as a man 'of good stature, *de buena estatura*', with a strong and well-made figure. 'And in his eyes,' he recalled, 'there was something kindly but also something grave.' His chaplain, Francisco López de Gómara, remembered him as elegant in his dress, and said he bore himself with gravity and prudence. The

Weiditz sketch confirmed those verbal portraits, and in the top right-hand corner of his drawing he wrote, in the High German of the sixteenth century, 'Cordeysus, 1529, at the age of forty-two [*sic*]: this man won all India for his Imperial Majesty Carlos V.'

There was a boy in the *Trachtenbuch*, but he was not Martín Cortés. In his hand-written caption Weiditz identified the child he had drawn as a servant to 'a rich prelate in Toledo'. I had thought, and had dared to hope, that Martín Cortés might have caught the eye of this eager artist, but I should have known better. He was his father's beloved son, not a specimen for display. In any case, by the time Weiditz made his careful sketches, Martín had been subsumed into the life of the royal court.

Santiago

O n a bleak afternoon in April, I walked shivering toward Madrid's Atocha railway station. The temperature gauge on the corner told me it was just four degrees Celsius. The Spanish capital in early spring was as cold as Mexico City in winter.

Inside the station, within the warmth of its palm garden, I waited for my train among Spaniards reading *El Pais* and Moroccans keeping to themselves. Otovalan 'Indians' from Ecuador sat wrapped in blue ponchos, golden beads around the women's necks, and not far from them a group of Mayans from Chiapas in southern Mexico stood silently beneath the palms. The people of the empire had come to make their own claim on Spain.

The station had once been a monastery, and the contours of the monks' cells were still visible in the walls around the waiting room. In one of them the first bishop of Chiapas had spent his final years. His name was Bartolomé de Las Casas. When he died his fellow Dominicans had to force his cell door open because a mountain of paper had accumulated behind it. Las Casas had died quill in hand, still denouncing Spain's conquests in the Americas as he had throughout his life. I was on my way north to Valladolid, a city he knew well.

There was snow on the dark peaks of the Sierra de Madrid and snowflakes drifting about the walls of Avila, where the mystic Teresa de Jesus had spent her life in prayer and ecstasy. After Avila a line of sleek white windmills crossed a high green ridge to the east, their shining blades turning slowly in the cold air, and just before Valladolid my train paused in Medina del Campo, where Bernal Diaz del Castillo was born and raised.

All his life he had loved the great chivalric romances of his day, like the *Tales of Amadis* and the *Ballad of Montesinos*, with their fantastical plots and their heroic conclusions. But when he was a boy growing up beneath Medina's old Moorish castle, surely not even he could have dreamed he would end his days with a Mayan wife and a cluster of mestizo children by his side, in a land he didn't yet know existed.

It was dusk by the time we reached Valladolid. I had not reserved a room, thinking I would arrive in time to wander and find a place to stay. I hadn't considered the icy air that would descend on the town as darkness fell, nor the possibility, explained to me by the first desk clerk I spoke to, that most rooms might be taken up by delegates to an economics conference. Valladolid is a quiet city and I knew I had nothing to fear if I couldn't find a bed — nothing except the cold, and the vexation of having to return to Madrid that night. But finally, in a plaza near the church of Santiago, I found a room in a small inn.

Later that evening, in a café across the plaza, I listened to the ladies of Valladolid talk through clouds of cigarette smoke about their shopping trips to Madrid and their holidays in Murcia. The Castillian clatter of their voices sounded very different from the gentle murmur of Mexican Spanish, and it was strange to hear them talk about their innocent pleasures, in such a place as this. Columbus had died alone and in poverty in Valladolid. Isabella of Castille had galloped here in secret at the age of seventeen to marry her even younger cousin, Ferdinand of Aragon, and forge a new nation out of their disparate Christian provinces. And here, in 1550, the formidable Dominican, Las Casas, had dared to tell the emperor, Carlos V, that Aristotle had been wrong in his doctrine of 'natural slavery'.

'All the peoples of the world are men,' Las Casas had insisted during his astonishing speech at Valladolid. 'Mankind is one,' he thundered, 'and all men are alike in that which concerns their creation.' His ideas were a fierce departure from the wisdom of the times, all the more so when we consider that Las Casas expounded his beliefs two centuries before Thomas Jefferson penned his own famous assertion of the equality of men.

Yet both those dazzling thinkers were guilty of a similar blindness toward one branch of the human family. When Jefferson wrote that all men were created equal he did not include African slaves in his concept of liberty. Las Casas too was initially guilty of that terrible exclusion, for in his anxiety to protect the people of the Americas from exploitation by their Spanish conquerors, he advocated African slavery instead. It was an error he soon came to regret.

The Archivo General de Simancas is housed in a castle on a hill outside Valladolid. I climbed the stone steps up to the footbridge, crossed the empty moat to the enormous door and entered. Inside the air was icy and I shuddered as I followed the signs to the reading room.

The great French historian, Fernand Braudel, said the kings and princes of the sixteenth-century Mediterranean saw themselves as actors in a mighty drama. To him the wars, the dynastic marriages, all the numerous events that consumed their days, were just the ephemera of history, 'a mere scattering of dust' compared with the greater movements of time and tide, of climate and geography, of social and economic systems. So was Carlos V suffering a delusion of grandeur when he established the royal archive at Simancas? The archive was an expression of his Renaissance mind but also, perhaps, of his accurate belief that scholars would one day seek the small, quotidian details of his family's life. Rightly or wrongly it is the 'ephemera' of the past, and the frailties and strengths and sins of those who lived it, that we seem to find eternally enticing.

In the reading room I explained to the director why I had come. I told her I believed the son of Hernán Cortés had been a page at the royal court of Carlos V, and I wanted, if I could, to confirm this story. She went to a bookshelf and pulled out a large index. It was a list of attendants in the royal houses. I stood beside her as she turned each page slowly and carefully until, on page 128, we came to 'Cortés, Martín: Second Marqués del Valle'.

She looked at me inquiringly.

'Is that him?' she asked.

'I'm not sure,' I said and we read on.

'Pageboy in the household of the empress from 1530 until her death,' the entry continued. 'Assigned after that to the same position in the house of the prince, Felipe, in which he served until May 1541. He was the son of Hernán Cortés, first Marqués del Valle.'

'I think that's the boy I'm looking for,' I told her. 'He was the son of Hernán Cortés, and the dates match his life exactly.'

I read the entry again.

'But I think there might be an error here,' I said.

I explained my problem.

'You see, Cortés had two sons called Martín,' I told her, 'one legitimate, the other illegitimate. The legitimate one became the second marqués, but it's his half-brother I'm trying to trace.'

My story sounded so absurd in that silent room that I feared she might think I was crazy. But she listened and nodded sympathetically.

'The people who prepare these indexes are not *Americanistas,*' she said, employing the Spanish term for scholars whose field is the Americas. 'They probably did not dream that Cortés had two sons with the same name. But then, who would?' she added with a wry smile.

She made a corrective note in the index. Then she glanced down the long, dark, silent gallery where researchers sat in pools of lamplight pouring over manuscripts. She took me to a table at the end of the room, by a high window looking out across the plains below, switched on the lamp and pulled out the chair for me.

'I'll send for your documents,' she said.

They came to me in bundles, but I am always anxious at such moments and hesitated before beginning. Finally I untied the string around the first package and lifted the protective cardboard to reveal the many layers of parchment beneath. The sheets were large, about thirty by forty-two centimetres, and each one had been folded in two to form four pages. It was a cold, dark morning, but their shapely letters, soft brown ink on cream parchment, seemed to glow in the lamplight.

Archival work requires an archeologist's patience: the same gentle sifting, careful measuring, the endless searching for tiny fragments that might contribute to some larger story. You must adapt your eye to the shape and slant, the loops and scrolls and abbreviations of each scribe's hand. The more ostentatious letters can seem indecipherable at first, while the work of less artistic scribes, even after five hundred years, is often gratifyingly clear.

The parchments in the first bundle concerned the empress, Isabel. The chickens, eels, lambs and cabbages she and her household had consumed had been listed, along with arithmetical calculations of their costs. I worked slowly, unfolding each parchment, deciphering it then replacing it in correct sequence so as not to hinder the work of the next scholar who might come to read it.

Beneath the penciled number '832' I found the heading 'Pages in Waiting to the Royal Household of the Empress'. I ran my eyes carefully, anxiously, down the list of boys, and on the second page I found his name. The scribe had spelled it 'Martyn' in a common variation of the day. It was a brief entry, a simple note, to confirm that the fees of Martín Cortés's tutor, one Diego Pérez de Vargas, had been paid in full. The scribe's letters were small and vertical, but the tutor

RECEIPT FROM MARTÍN'S TUTOR
Archivo General di Simancas

had signed his name with a long, ornate flourish that stretched the entire width of the entry.

A few parchments later I found a similar receipt. 'I, Diego Pérez de Vargas,' it read, 'tutor to don Martyn Cortés … confirm that I have this day received fees in full for my services to the said don Martyn Cortés …' Pérez de Vargas had signed the document with that same elaborate signature and this time he had dated it. 'In Madrid,' he had written, 'the first of September, fifteen hundred and thirty.' Martín Cortés was eight years old by then.

I spent a long day folding and unfolding, sorting and reading. I found the document dealing with Martín's transfer to the prince's household. The sheet had been written in brown ink, in a clear sloping hand, and it too was a receipt of sorts, an inventory of the empress's pageboys who had recently been transferred to her son, Felipe. 'Of the pages formerly with our lady the empress,' it was headed, 'the following are now received.' A tragedy lay beneath that mundane entry because in 1539 Isabel had died in childbirth, leaving her husband and surviving children to mourn her loss.

Martín's name appeared on the second page. 'Don Martyn Cortés,' I read, 'son of the Marquis of the Valley, *hijo del Marqués del Valle*'. Seventy boys were listed in total and their entries reflected the glory of their aristocratic lineages. The grandson of the Count of Miranda was there, so was the son of the Duke of Infantado, and the son of the Duke of Medina Sidonia. So Malinche's child had lived in illustrious company at the royal court, but his father's new title looked strange and exotic beside those older, long-established ones.

I sat back in my chair by the window and looked out across the green plains of Old Castille. In the distance cars and trucks moved south along the highway toward Madrid, the drone of their engines silenced by the impenetrable castle walls around me. I had spent years searching for traces of Martín's mother, Malinche, finding little to assist me in the official records. Yet here was her child, listed as a page, just as I had hoped. It had to be him. His brother of the same name had not been born in 1530 when the entries commenced, and did not arrive in Spain until 1540, a year after the empress died.

Bernal Diaz del Castillo said that during the Conquest, Malinche had become close to a boy called Juan de Ortega, who was a page to Cortés. She had taught this boy the Aztec language, Náhuatl, and his proficiency was such, Diaz del Castillo said, that the emperor, Moctezuma, liked to talk with him. I wondered whether Malinche had understood, when her son left for Spain, that he too might become a page.

At the royal court Martín Cortés was not exposed to the terrors of the Conquest, as Juan de Ortega had been. Martín would have slept in vast dormitories with all those other boys from noble families who were his fellow pages, and eaten with them at long refectory tables in palaces and castles in Valladolid, in Barcelona, in Toledo and Madrid. Like them he would have dressed in fine clothes, and received rigorous instruction in Latin and Spanish beneath the watchful eye of the master of pages. He is certain to have heard the famous court preacher, Antonio de Guevara, read from his popular *Golden Book of Marcus Aurelius*, which examined the Stoic ideals of the great philosopher-emperor in seven hundred pages of highly ornate language. And Martín would have learned the art of sword-fighting, the importance of self-discipline, the skills required for the warrior's life he would have to lead.

So had his younger brother come to join him at the royal court at some point? The second Marqués del Valle was later said to have been a personal friend of Felipe, and service as a page was the usual pathway to friendship with a prince, so it seemed possible. It would explain the way their identities had been blended in the index. If it were true, the documents relating to the younger Martín Cortés must lie somewhere else in the archives.

Two days later I returned to Madrid to look into the faces of the men and women Malinche's child had served during his years as a page at the royal court.

In the Museo del Prado I saw Carlos V as Titian had painted him in Bologna at the age of thirty-two. He looked every inch an emperor with his proud posture and his

CARLOS V BY TITIAN, 1532

Reproduced with permission of Museo Nacional del Prado, Madrid

ISABEL, THE EMPRESS. POSTHUMOUS
PORTRAIT BY TITIAN

*Reproduced with permission of Museo Nacional
del Prado, Madrid*

hunting dog by his side. I saw his son, Felipe — a thin, uncertain young man in shining black armor — and I saw Felipe's mother, the beautiful sad-faced empress, Isabel, to whom Martín Cortés had been an attendant.

She had led a solitary life as spouse of the Holy Roman Emperor. She is said to have eaten alone and in silence

FELIPE II BY TITIAN

Reproduced with permission of Museo Nacional del Prado, Madrid

during the many long years Carlos V was away from Spain on imperial business in Augsburg or Milan or Lombardy. During her first labor she had gasped that she might die, but she would never scream, and she was true to her word. That first long and painful childbirth did not kill her. It was the third that did.

After their amicable first meeting late in 1528, Carlos V returned to Hernán Cortés the estates the Crown had confiscated while he was in Honduras. Carlos also granted Cortés perpetual rights to them, in a rare concession he gave to only one other person: Isabel Moctezuma, the daughter of the Aztec emperor. All other conquistadors in Mexico, except Cortés, would be forced to surrender their estates after two generations, for Carlos, like his grandparents Isabella and Ferdinand, was determined to prevent the rise of a hereditary feudal nobility.

His resolve caused a bitter division in conquistador society, one into which Malinche's child would be drawn on his return to Mexico. But that was not for some years yet. In the meantime the emperor continued to treat Hernán Cortés handsomely. He refused to make him viceroy of the land he had conquered however. It was the thing Cortés desired above all else, but Carlos reserved that critical role for a trusted member of the aristocratic Mendoza family.

Later that week in the Archivo Historico Nacional as I waited for some documents to come to me, I took an encyclopedia of genealogy from the bookshelf and turned to the entry for 'Cortés'.

It was a habit I had fallen into, of checking to see whether the first-born Martín Cortés was included in the family tree. Sometimes he was missing altogether, incorporated accidentally into the identity of his legitimate younger brother, as if he had never existed. This time a different kind of fusion had occurred. 'Natural children,' I read, '*hijos naturales*': 'Martín Cortés Moctezuma, begotten by doña Isabel Moctezuma, daughter of the emperor Moctezuma. He [don Martín] was a knight of the Order of Santiago.'

It was the first time I had seen Malinche's child confused with Moctezuma's son, who had sailed with him from Mexico, but it was an understandable error. They had arrived in Spain together, and both were sons of Amerindian mothers. Isabel Moctezuma had indeed borne a child to Hernán Cortés not long before he left for Spain — a little girl called Leonor — but Martín Cortés Moctezuma, or Martín Cortés Nezahualzolotl as he was also known, was Isabel's brother, not her son.

Someone else had noted the mistake. In a neat hand, in pencil, in the margin, he or she had deleted the word 'Moctezuma' from Martín's name and written 'Falso! He was the son of doña Marina, la Malintzin.' Yes, I murmured to the scholar who had visited this page before me, he was

Malinche's child. And it was he, not his Aztec namesake, who was a knight of Santiago. That was why I had come to the Archivo Historico — to read the documents relating to his membership of that illustrious military order.

The archivist caught my eye. I closed the encyclopedia and went forward to collect the slender folder he held out to me. It had been tied with white cotton tape, and on its cover I saw the red sword-cross of the Order of Santiago. At the end of a long table in the sunlit reading room I opened it and found the testimonies of four men who, in July 1529, had gone to Toledo to give evidence that seven-year-old Martín Cortés was worthy to be admitted to the Order of Santiago.

One of them I knew, or thought I did. He had been with Martín's parents from the earliest moments of the Conquest. His name was Diego de Ordaz. In November 1519 he had climbed the great snowcapped volcano Popocatépetl and from its crater had become the first European to see the Aztec city of Tenochtitlán in the valley below. Bernal Diaz del Castillo had described him as 'brave and judicious with something of a stammer' and this conquistador who stuttered had long intrigued me. Was it hard, I wondered, for such a man to speak formally and publicly before a panel of learned men in Toledo? Were they less or more formidable than an erupting volcano and a city brimming with Aztec warriors?

Whatever it took for him to do so, Diego de Ordaz stammered out his testimony in Toledo, declaring that he had known don Martín Cortés for six years, and that the boy was the son of don Hernándo Cortés and doña Marina, a 'principal Indian' of Guazacualco. Like all Spaniards, Ordaz called Malinche by her Spanish name, 'Marina', and referred to the region where she was born as 'Guazacualco' rather than 'Coatzacoalcos'. She had played a vital role in the discovery of New Spain, he said, and was married now to a Spaniard called Juan Xaramillo. So in 1529 she was still alive and living in her husband's house a few blocks north of the plaza in Mexico City.

Three other witnesses followed Diego de Ordaz, and they too had taken part in the Conquest. There were variations in the spelling the scribes employed as they recorded their testimonies — 'Martín' occasionally became 'Martyn', 'Marina' was sometimes 'Maryna' — but their evidence was more or less unanimous. That did not surprise me. Candidates were entitled to select their own witnesses, and Hernán Cortés would have chosen these four carefully, on his son's behalf.

The Order of Santiago, or St James, was descended from the old monastic fraternities like the Templars and the Hospitallers founded in Jerusalem during the Crusades. But Santiago was quintessentially Spanish because the saint it commemorated was famed for his mythological role in a great defeat against Islamic forces on Spanish soil during the ninth century.

That spring, as I traveled through Spain, I saw the sword-like cross of Santiago gleaming red through stained-glass windows across the country. In Madrid, in the Museo del Prado, I noticed it on the breast of the painter, Diego Velázquez, in his self-portrait in 'Las Meninas'. In an effigy in Sigüenza the sword-cross decorated the tunic of a pageboy killed in battle against the Moors of Granada. The prestige of the Order can be appreciated when we realise that Carlos V himself was its head.

Aspirants to the Order were obliged to attend their hearings, so Martín Cortés must have sat through the proceedings in Toledo, a small figure listening silently as his father's friends confirmed that he was a boy of virtuous nature and sound mental capacity, and that the Amerindian mother he did not know was a 'principal Indian' of good character and standing. The master and the prior of the Order listened too, and it seems they found the child satisfactory on all counts because they admitted him to their ranks as a knight of the Order of Santiago.

The admission ceremony required him to lie on the cool, tiled floor and listen as the eighty clauses of the Order's rules on fasting and poverty, on charity toward captives, on one's duty to make war on the Infidel, were read aloud to him, in Latin. Martín Cortés would have known Latin. It would have been an essential part of his schooling in the house of Juan Altamirano, and would have continued to be so at the royal court. He may not have known that warrior codes had existed in Tenochtitlán as well as in Toledo, however; and that had he been born in the Aztec city a few years earlier and, to different parents, he might have been an eagle or a jaguar knight and dedicated his life to war against his neighboring city states rather than the Infidel.

I wondered whether the officials of the Order had prepared a child-size robe for Martín Cortés when the time came to dress him in the white habit of Santiago. Or had they draped a man's cloak and tunic around his small body, knowing he would grow into it eventually? Either way the red sword-cross of Santiago would have been displayed across his heart, as it was on the breast of the valiant page-boy who had died in Granada.

Martín Cortés was seven years old. As a child raised among Spaniards he would have understood the significance of Santiago, and may have sensed, as children do, his father's anxiety to see him succeed where he had not for, after the Conquest, Cortés had tried and failed to become a knight of Santiago. The reasons for his rejection are unknown, but the Order required its members to display, outwardly at least, chastity and obedience, and in those two essential virtues Cortés, with his independent character and his well-known passion for women, would have been seen to have conspicuously failed.

A few days after Martín Cortés was admitted to the Order of Santiago, his father married for the second time.

It was a brilliant and surprising match for a man like Hernán Cortés for his bride was the niece of the Duke of Bejar, who was a godfather to the three-year-old prince, Felipe. I knew from Cortés's letters that his father had worked tirelessly to promote this marriage before he died, yet the influence the elder Martín Cortés had brought to the matrimonial negotiations was never clear. He was not an aristocrat, but he is said to have come from Salamanca, which was close to Bejar's ancestral home, so perhaps an old provincial allegiance gave him access to the duke. Or perhaps they shared some now-forgotten association through Alonso de Monroy, the noble rebel to whom the first Martín Cortés is said to have been related.

We know far more about the Duke of Bejar. Prior to Carlos V's wedding four years earlier, this royal favorite had been sent to the Portuguese border to greet the empress-to-be, Isabel, and conduct her to Seville. The duke is said to have arrived at the frontier with eighteen pages and thirteen musicians and, as this princess of Portugal crossed into Spain with her brothers, to have leaped from his horse to kiss her hand. His contemporaries spoke in awe of his lavish sleeves trailing the floor at royal suppers, of his long gown trimmed with gold and pearls and precious stones. A French visitor to Valladolid saw him sweep by in a gown of crimson velvet, lined with cloth of silver and sewn with tiny pillars of pure gold.

Whatever ancient loyalties lay behind the prelude to his niece's marriage, it is clear that a man like Bejar required a fortune to sustain such expensive tastes, and the allure of

New World riches that now followed Hernán Cortés wherever he went can only have enhanced his eligibility in the duke's eyes.

The bride's name was Juana Ramirez de Arellano y Zúñiga, but these days she is referred to more simply as Juana de Zúñiga. I had seen a marble bust of her years earlier in the palace in Mexico where she and Hernán Cortés went to live. She had looked delicate and pale with her downcast eyes and her pursed lips, yet her fragility must have been an illusion for she is almost the only woman in this story who lives long enough to raise her children to adulthood.

She is always described as young when she married Cortés. She may have been anywhere between sixteen and twenty. Her feelings toward this older stranger to whom her uncle had betrothed her are unknown, but they would have been irrelevant to her destiny. Like all aristocratic European daughters at that time she lived in a gilded cage, a hostage to her family's acquisitive dynastic plans.

Women seemed to find Cortés attractive, however, and in this doña Juana may have been no different from his many lovers in Cuba and in Mexico. Bernal Diaz del Castillo said

JUANA DE ZÚÑIGA, STEPMOTHER OF MARTÍN CORTÉS
Museo de Cuauhnahuac, Cuernavaca, Mexico

Cortés was excessively fond of women. Francisco López de Gómara agreed that he always gave himself to them. It may be that he returned to Spain with a warrior's glamor, and a charm that a pampered noblewoman like Juana de Zúñiga might find appealing.

I wondered whether she knew about the death of his first wife seven years earlier, and that he had been accused of murdering her. Or had doña Juana's family concealed the stories from her? Did she know that in marrying Cortés she was acquiring four step-children, one of whom was the grand-daughter of the late Aztec emperor?

None of this may have concerned her, for aristocratic households in sixteenth-century Spain were not the small and private units families have become today, and illegitimate children were not usually excluded from them. Whatever doña Juana knew, whatever her fears or regrets or personal desires, in July 1529 she became the first Marquesa del Valle and step-mother to Malinche's child.

Late that summer of 1529 the Aztec members of Cortés's retinue began the first stage of their journey home to Mexico. They went south to Seville, and while they waited for the ship that would carry them back across the Atlantic, handsome garments were prepared for them at the emperor's expense and to his exact specifications.

Nobles like don Martín Cortés Nezahualzolotl and his half-brother, don Pedro Gutierrez Aculan Moctezuma, were given blue velvet jerkins and caps, doublets of yellow damask, capes and breeches of scarlet cloth, ribboned shoes and leather gaiters. Commoners like Gabriel Tecpal and Julian Quauhpiltzintli received yellow cloth jerkins, white cotton doublets, mulberry capes and scarlet caps.

But death stalked the exotic visitors as they waited for a ship to Mexico, for several of them died suddenly in quick succession. The malady that killed them is unclear, but it could have been small pox, chicken pox, mumps, influenza or any number of afflictions. No European illness was so trivial that it could not kill a Native American.

In retrospect, given their susceptibility, it seems miraculous that any of them survived to make the voyage back to Mexico. Yet most did survive. They battled their illnesses, mourned their dead companions and wondered about the fate of their fellow Aztec, a dancer called Benito Matlequeni, who had gone to Rome to see the pope and had fallen ill there. They waited in Seville for his return, and for the ship to take them home, and while they waited Moctezuma's son, that other Martín Cortés, took a Spanish wife. Her name was never recorded, but when he sailed for Mexico in August she sailed with him.

In Spain I learned that almost everything Hernán Cortés desired for his first-born son was something that had once been denied to him. Cortés had secured Martín a position as page at the royal court; he had seen him admitted to the Order of Santiago. There was one more privilege he wanted for him before he returned to Mexico and the lands the emperor had now restored to him. He wanted Martín legitimized.

Legitimacy could be granted or, more correctly, purchased by papal decree. Cortés knew this and had already dispatched an attorney to Rome to ensure Martín would not be burdened with the stain of illegitimacy for the rest of his life. The attorney was now on his way back to Spain, carrying a precious papal bull declaring that Martín Cortés, together with another half-brother and half-sister in Mexico whom he did not yet know, were now legitimate.

'To our beloved sons, Martín Cortés and Luis de Altamirano,' the pope, Clemente VII had written, 'and to our beloved daughter, Catalina Pizarro, of the diocese of Mexico … children of our beloved son, Fernando Cortés, good health and apostolic blessing.' The pope assured Martín Cortés and his siblings that the vice of illegitimate birth in no way tarnished their brightness, because the beauty of their virtue would cleanse them of the stain of their birth, while their pure conduct would erase the shame of their origins.

He noted that their father had asked with great humility that his children be legitimized, therefore he, Clemente VII, had decided to use his apostolic authority to cleanse them of every mark or stain of illegitimacy, and restore to them the ancient rights of legitimate birth. 'And I declare,' Clemente concluded, 'that you are legitimate and that in this no other laws, neither imperial nor municipal, take precedence over apostolic law.'

The pope himself was illegitimate. He had been born Giulio de Medici and as a nephew of Lorenzo the Magnificent he never suffered for his birth. His portrait in the Vatican Museum shows a slender man with black hair, deep brown eyes and fine elegant features, impossibly young, improbably handsome for a pontiff. 'A typical Medici' his contemporaries called him. He too had an illegitimate child to whom he seems to have been deeply attached — a son, Alessandro, whose mother was an African servant girl. This nineteen-year-old African-Italian Medici was already Duke of Penna.

He would soon be Duke of Florence and husband to the daughter of Carlos V, so neither his African blood, nor his illegitimacy had disadvantaged him.

As a cardinal Clemente VII had been the patron of Niccolò Machiavelli. As pontiff he would spend his apostolic reign grappling with the earth-shaking tremors of the Reformation, and the demands of Martin Luther of Germany and Henry Tudor of England. His love for his own son may have persuaded this last Medici pope to look kindly on Martín Cortés, but legitimizing Malinche's child was also one of the simplest requests he had to face during his tumultuous reign. For Hernán Cortés, however, it was a complex and costly process: he had to pay for his attorney's long journey to Rome and back, and the expenses of his stay there. He had to pay the fees the Vatican demanded for the privilege of legitimization. Why, apart from a natural love for his children, was this formality so important to him?

Spanish and Portuguese aristocrats had often recognized their illegitimate children in this way, and an ambitious man like Hernán Cortés must have taken pride in his ability to follow their lordly tradition. But there were other considerations. In 1529, when he sent his attorney to Rome to see the pope, he was forty-four years old in an age when men were fortunate to live until fifty. He had now acquired a new young wife, but he had no way of knowing whether she would give him any children.

His dread that his name might disappear seems to have haunted Cortés throughout his life. In that letter of September 1526 to his father he had said he would rather be rich in fame than in worldly goods. And when the twentieth-century Spanish historian, Salvador de Madariaga, wrote his elegiac biography of Cortés he noticed something the conqueror had said in another of his melancholy letters, this time in the last one he wrote to Carlos V. 'If daughters succeed,' Cortés had told the emperor, 'memory is lost.'

War is Thy Destiny

Malinche's child was eight years old when his father left him at the royal court of Spain. Two years later, on the twelfth of June 1532, his mother's Spanish husband, Juan Xaramillo, lodged a *probanza*, or proof of services, with the vice-regal authorities in Mexico. In it Xaramillo described himself as married, *casado y velado*, to doña Beatriz de Andrade. So Malinche must have been dead by then; had died, perhaps in one of the epidemics devastating Mexico at that time, or in childbirth, like so many other women of that time. It is possible her child, Martín, knew nothing of her passing — that no-one thought to tell him — for he had been separated from her for several years now.

Later that same year of 1532 the half-brother who would share his name was born in Mexico. When and how

Malinche's child received the news of his brother's arrival in the world is not recorded. Perhaps his tutor told him, or he may have heard it through the gossiping circles of the court. There was no reason to conceal this information from him, or to deliver it with cautious discretion as families might today. In sixteenth-century Europe, where war and epidemic disease touched everyone, and childbearing took women's lives with terrible frequency, step-families were the rule rather than the exception.

In Mexico Juana de Zúñiga had survived her first labor, but the twins she bore did not. 'The son and daughter given to us by God have died,' Hernán Cortés told his cousin in Spain, Francisco de Nuñez, in a letter of June 1532. The dead children had been baptized Luis and Catalina — the same names Cortés had previously given to the son and daughter legitimized with Malinche's child. But Cortés told his cousin there was hope, despite his children's deaths, for doña Juana 'was pregnant again, *aora está preñada*'.

Later that year, as if in answer to his prayers, she gave birth to a second boy. Cortés, for whom male children and 'memory' meant so much, rejoiced at the safe delivery of this son by his aristocratic wife and called the boy 'Martín Cortés' after his beloved father. He continued his repetitive naming habits, and set in motion the curious and often confusing dualities of this family story.

Around the time his half-brother came into the world, the first Martín, Malinche's child, fell ill in Spain. When Cortés learned of his sickness he wrote again to his cousin in words that still burn with anxiety and indignation.

'With your letter of October,' he tells Nuñez, 'you sent a note from Diego Pérez de Vargas with an account of don Martín's illness. You said that you would go and see about it and write to me with the truth, but I have seen no letter of yours ... You may well believe that the news of his illness caused me pain, and perhaps you didn't wish to write to me about it.' He seems to pause here, to ensure his meaning is clear. 'Well,' he thunders, 'I want you to know that I do not love him less than the child God has given me through the marquesa, and that I therefore desire to know everything of him, always ...'

It is strangely moving to hear the conqueror of Mexico reduced to trembling anguish like this over his child. Strange to hear him lose the careful composure with which he wrote his famous letters to the emperor. Months have passed since he first learned that Martín was ill, ships have come and gone between Spain and Mexico, but he has heard nothing more. It is obvious he fears his cousin does not understand the depth of his feelings for this child. Has Martín perished? Will nobody tell him the truth?

'Write to me as quickly as possible about his health,' he begs his cousin, 'because since receiving the account you sent I have had no relief from my anxiety.'

'It affected me deeply,' he continues, 'that it was said his illness was *lamparones*. I think that is the greatest falsehood in the world, because the child has a good constitution and what he has must be *pujamiento de sangre*, which could have been cured at the beginning by taking him to the country.' *Lamparones*? A diminutive of *lampara* or 'lamp'? What could 'little lamps' have meant in sixteenth-century medical terms? And *pujamiento de sangre*? The pushing of blood? Why does Cortés sound so angry about the alleged nature of his son's illness?

In Spain that spring I learned that *lamparones* signified the disease the French and the English called 'the king's evil' because they believed a king could cure it. In *Macbeth*, the Scottish prince, Malcolm, describes its sufferers as 'strangely visited people, all swollen and ulcerous, pitiful to the eye.'

In modern medical terms it is known as 'scrofula', but it is seldom encountered in the Western world these days. It is a form of tuberculosis that attacks the lymph nodes in the neck, causing abscess and ulceration of the skin. So there was a terrible logic to the expression 'little lamps' to describe the burning ulcers on Martín Cortés's neck.

Whereas *lamparones* was a wretched and disfiguring condition, *pujamiento de sangre* was a respectable malady. In the medical wisdom of the day it denoted an excess of one of the essential 'humors', in this case, blood. It was an illness that might be cured by taking the afflicted person to the fresh air of the countryside. These notions of acceptable and unacceptable illness, familiar to us still, must explain Cortés's indignation at his son's diagnosis. He believed his child had been wrongly labeled with an abhorrent disease and, if that were not bad enough, had been deprived of the correct medical treatment for his true condition.

Had Martín Cortés been resident at the royal court of England his king may well have laid his hands on him in an attempt at cure. But in 1532 the emperor was in Augsburg or Brussels or Piedmont, on imperial business as usual, for he was rarely in Spain. Even if Carlos V had been at court that year, Spain's rulers did not claim the healing powers attributed to the English and the French monarchs. So how was Martín Cortés's illness treated? A court surgeon was probably called to lance his ulcerous buboes, and from that day on his neck would have shown the scars such treatment caused.

There are other suggestive allusions in this letter of 1532. 'Apart from the money I have already sent you,' Cortés continues, 'I have now sent another five hundred pesos to the Lord Count of Miranda, and entrusted the child to him, so he can handle the matter of the tutor's fees ...' Is he implying here that Martín's tutor has failed in his duty of care because of some dispute over money? Perhaps, although it is impossible to know for certain without an understanding of what is troubling Cortés. But there is nothing ambiguous in the way he declares his feelings for his ailing son. When he tells his cousin he does not love Martín less than his newborn son, and demands to know everything about him, his words still ring with the passion of a father deeply and insistently attached to his first-born child.

It is painful now to think of ten-year-old Martín Cortés 'swollen and ulcerous, pitiful to the eye', enduring his illness without a parent or a loving relative by his side. But at ten he was no longer a child in sixteenth-century terms, and he would have been expected to bear his sufferings with silent courage, like any other boy of his time and place.

He was still at court five years later because in 1537 Hernán Cortés wrote to Carlos V to seek a position as page for his son, Luis, and in his letter he made reference to Martín. 'Sacra Católica Cesarea Majestad,' he begins with the usual formalities, 'As I cannot personally reside in your service I am sending this son to be with the one already there, to serve your Majesty and the prince. He is well educated for his age and is a virtuous child. I ask that Your Majesty receive him and grant him favors.'

The first-born Martín did not yet know his half-brother, this 'virtuous child' who had been legitimized with him in 1529 and who, although he was referred to in the papal bull as Luis de Altamirano, was known throughout his life as Luis Cortés. It would be some time before these brothers met, for in a letter to his cousin two years later Cortés mentioned that 'don Luis' was still with him in Mexico, as was 'don Martín', his youngest son. Meanwhile the first Martín, Malinche's child, remained alone in Spain, serving the royal court 'in the realms of Castille'.

It was a coveted existence for a boy of that time, but daily life in those early boarding schools was harsh by modern Western standards. Martín Cortés and his fellow pages lived at the mercy of their tutors, and without the parental nurturing we now consider essential. Aldo Scaglione tells us in his *Knights at Court* that reticence was considered an admirable virtue in a courtier. Martín Cortés would later be described as a reticent man.

Scaglione also said that courtiers lived in a rarefied atmosphere of conscious self-fashioning. It was a self-fashioning in which chivalry and manners were considered the two essential civilizing forces, and in which knights and courtiers asked themselves, insistently and constantly, 'Who am I?' I wondered if the young Martín Cortés had ever asked himself that critical question? If so, what did he reply? He was the only mestizo resident at the court of Carlos V, although others would follow later. Was there a moment when, like the *petit monstre* in Oscar Wilde's moving story *The Birthday of the Infanta*, he caught sight of himself in a mirror and saw that he was not quite like those around him?

Aztec women thought of childbirth as a bloody battle. 'This is our kind of war,' they sang in one of their hymns. 'Is this not a fatal time for us poor women?' Like their European sisters they knew that labor and its aftermath was a perilous time. They knew that was when the goddess Cihuacoatl came to collect her tribute of death from them. In Spain in May 1539 the empress Isabel lost her woman's war when she gave birth to a stillborn infant, and died a few days later. Her husband, Carlos V, retreated in sorrow to a monastery, and her twelve-year-old son, Felipe, fell ill, perhaps out of grief for the mother he had suddenly lost.

Isabel's pages were obliged to walk with her coffin from Toledo to the royal tombs at Granada where Queen Isabella and King Ferdinand lay buried. We know that Martín Cortés was still at court because in a document Hernán Cortés composed in Mexico that year he referred to him as 'don Martín my natural son, who is a servant of the prince, don Felipe, el principe, don Phelype, Nuestro Señor, in the realms of Castille.' So Malinche's child must have walked with the other royal attendants in that forlorn procession to Granada.

The cortege took eighteen days to reach its destination, which was far too long in the increasing warmth of spring. The empress's body had been embalmed with myrrh and aloe, and her casket scented with musk, but by the time the Duke of Gandia, Francisco de Borja, whose grandson would one day marry an Inca princess, opened it in Granada for the purposes of formal identification, her corpse had collapsed into a stinking horror. He later said that it was the sight of her putrefying cadaver that inspired him to relinquish his title and his riches and adopt the life of Jesuit austerity for which he was known thereafter.

The death of an empress required that her jewels and garments be distributed to family members or sold at public auction. This was done and her attendants were moved to other positions in the royal houses. So it was in this grief-stricken atmosphere that Martín was transferred to the household of the bereaved Felipe, who was five years his junior.

Martín Cortés was now seventeen. He had been at court for almost ten years, but apart from those brief references to him in the royal archives and in his father's letters and documents, we know little of his time there. What did he look like at seventeen? I think of him as a boy like any boy one might see in Mexico City today: slightly built, with coal-black hair, an aquiline nose, copper skin and almond eyes, but with tell-tale scarring around his neck as a reminder of his battle with disease. A silent boy who walked with the elegance and grace required of a young courtier. A boy accustomed to the rich formality and ritual of the imperial court.

He was not a royal child like the prince he now served, and he was still too young and insignificant to have commissioned a portrait, or even a miniature, of himself. But in the Museo del Prado one grey morning I found a small reproduction of the famous portrait Velázquez had made in 1650 of his studio assistant, Juan de Pareja. Pareja was a Spaniard of Berber ancestry, not the mestizo child of an Amerindian mother. Yet something in his direct and solemn gaze made me think of Martín Cortés.

One year after Martín Cortés was transferred to the prince's household, his father, Hernán Cortés, returned to Spain for the last time. How did Martín greet him after ten years apart — with delight, with sorrow, or with surprise? Their emotions, their words, the embraces they exchanged are not recorded. At fifty-six Cortés was old for his time, and weary from his political struggles with the emperor's viceroy, who he always believed had usurped his rightful place in Mexico. The letters Cortés had written to Carlos V since his return to Mexico in 1530 reveal an old conquistador who still felt unrewarded for his great conquest, a man still yearning for his emperor's approval and esteem. This time Cortés brought no

Aztec princes, no acrobats, no ocelots or jaguars with him to Spain, but he did bring his two younger sons: Luis, the middle brother, and the second-born Martín, who was now eight years old.

So at the age of eighteen and in his father's company, the first-born Martín Cortés finally met the brother who was his twin in name, if not in age. What did they make of each other, these half-brothers with the same father, the same name, but very different mothers? I did not yet know, although later, back in Mexico, I would begin to understand. But in 1540 Malinche's child had little time left at the royal court for, according to the records at Simancas, in May the following year he left the prince's service. It was a very specific date and I knew where he had gone.

The French historian, Fernand Braudel, said that war punctuated the sixteenth-century Mediterranean year with its rhythms, opening and closing the gates of time with terrible regularity. It is a good analogy. When sixteenth-century Europeans were not fighting other Europeans or invading the Americas — although this was still a very minor part of their military activities — they were fighting the Infidel armies of that other great emperor of the time, Suleyman the Magnificent. By 1541 his Ottoman Empire had coiled itself around the Mediterranean like a serpent. It had spread east from the rim of Austria, across the Balkans to Greece and Turkey, down through Palestine to Egypt and west across North Africa to Oran in present-day Algeria; it had almost encircled Spain.

Spaniards had long endured a sense of vulnerable geography, for slavery in North Africa was a common fate for coastal dwellers and seafarers captured by corsairs from across the Strait of Gibraltar. Cervantes himself, the soon-to-be-born creator of *Don Quixote*, would one day be a slave in Algiers. But since the fall of Granada in 1492, Christian Spaniards had also come to fear the enemy within they had created when they forced Islamic Spaniards to convert to Christianity. They now suspected these hapless converts of collaborating with the enemy across the straits in North Africa.

In 1535 Carlos V had captured the city of Tunis. In May 1541 he turned his attention to Algiers. His imperial fleet of German, Italian and Spanish galleys began gathering at the island of Mallorca. In October this vast armed flotilla sailed due south to North Africa. Hernán Cortés was among the Spaniards who embarked on this great adventure, and Martín Cortés, who was now nineteen, sailed with him.

Malinche's son had been raised among the nobility of Spain, but he had no land or wealth to call his own. The soldier's life was the only honorable path for him to follow. As a child initiate of the Order of Santiago he had vowed to fight the Infidel. Now, as a young man, the opportunity to keep that promise as a member of such a noble imperial mission against the eternal Islamic enemy, with his father by his side, must have seemed irresistible.

The confusion regarding the brothers called Martín Cortés begins in earnest in the contemporary records of the Algerian campaign. Cortés's chaplain and biographer, Francisco López de Gómara, said that don Luis and don Martín went with Cortés to Algiers, but he did not say which don Martín. Bernal Diaz del Castillo said both boys called Martín took part in the expedition and he was quite specific about this. He said that Cortés took his son 'who inherited the estate', as well as 'don Martín Cortés whom he had by doña Marina, *el que hubo con doña Marina*'.

Twenty-five years later, under interrogation in Mexico, Malinche's child would confirm under oath that he had indeed gone to Algiers that spring. But did his younger brother of the same name go with him, as Bernal Diaz del Castillo believed? In 1541 the second-born Martín Cortés was only nine, but that was old enough in sixteenth-century Europe to go to war. Boys carried their lords' banners into battle, attended them in every way they could, and sometimes they died, as the valiant pageboy in Granada had died. So Diaz del Castillo may well have been correct to say that the younger Martín also went to Algiers. I never found any evidence to confirm that this was true, however. The only certainty is that in the spring of 1541 Hernán Cortés, his first-born son, Martín, and his middle son, Luis, sailed toward Algiers in a fine galley called *Esperanza*.

Its name meant hope. But the expedition proved a disaster for the Christian forces. Before they could engage in battle a tempest smashed their fleet against the jagged coast of North Africa, and Carlos V, the 'first and last great emperor of Europe' who loved war and had never known defeat, learned that failure was possible, even for him, and ordered a general retreat.

Hernán Cortés's response to his emperor's decision to withdraw has been retold so many times that it has become one of the famous set-pieces of Cortésian history. Both Diaz del Castillo and López de Gómara tell us that Cortés was so appalled by the idea of retreat that he came forward and offered to take Algiers with the remaining forces. To him the tempest and the shipwrecks were merely a temporary setback — a strategic problem to be solved. He was an ageing soldier, however, and few people knew who he was or what he had achieved in Mexico. His bold proposal came to nothing, and Bernal Diaz del Castillo said that Cortés lamented out loud that he did not have under his command the soldiers who had taken the Aztec city of Tenochtitlán with him twenty years earlier. They were men, he said, who could suffer hunger and ordeals and storms or whatever came their way, and still perform heroic deeds. They were men whose injuries never prevented them from fighting on and capturing fortresses and pyramids and cities.

Cortés may have said all this, and news of his speech may well have reached the ears of Diaz del Castillo, who was by then on his way to a new life in Guatemala. But the words he places in Cortés's mouth may also reflect his own old conquistador's disdain for a younger generation of men who could be forced into retreat by a mere storm. They are words he must have longed to believe his former commander had uttered, loudly and with dignity, in the hearing of doña Marina's child on the rocky coast of North Africa.

And how did the nineteen-year-old Martín Cortés experience this travesty of an invasion as he fought for his life in the waters of the Mediterranean? It was not an auspicious beginning to his career as a warrior, but he had survived while twelve thousand other men had not. Was he proud of his father's courage? Did he feel angry, or embarrassed by the fact that Cortés was now a forgotten man? Or did he believe in him when no-one else did? Whatever he felt, he, his father and at least one of his brothers, found a place on one of the remaining vessels, and by November 1541 they had returned to the safety of Spanish waters.

Circles of Confusion

I lost sight of Malinche's son for a while after Algiers. But I knew that a *probanza*, or proof of service to the Crown his own son had made in 1592, resided in the archives in Seville. So I went south to that languorous city by the river Guadalquivir, to the Archivo General de Indias, to see what, if anything, that manuscript could tell me about Martín Cortés.

The son's name was Fernando. Martín had named him after his father who, although we remember him as 'Hernán', was more often known as Fernando or Hernando, even occasionally Ferdinando, in his lifetime. The younger Fernando Cortés had lodged his *probanza* in Peru. He had gone there, he said, as a member of the Count of Villar's retinue. He described himself as the son of 'don Martyn

Cortés, Knight of the Order of Santiago and gentleman of his Catholic Majesty the King, don Phelipe Segundo'. Fernando did not give his mother's name, and may never have known it. Her absence from his story puzzled me until, a few days later, I discovered that he had been born out of wedlock, and raised in his father's household.

I never learned Fernando's mother's name. She may have been a family servant, or a village girl, or even a noblewoman who gave birth to their child in secret and then relinquished him to Martín's care. Sixteenth-century Spanish men could acknowledge their illegitimate children without fear for their reputation, but women could not, therefore the identity of Fernando's mother is lost to history. We know only that at some point Martín Cortés had been her lover, and that she had borne a child to him. Her name, her age, her origins, the place where she gave birth to their son, whether or not she survived her labor — none of these details have surfaced in the Cortés family records.

Fernando knew who his paternal grandparents were, however. He identified them as 'don Fernando Cortés, the first Marqués del Valle', and 'doña Marina Cortés, *yndia natural* of the kingdoms of New Spain', giving her a family name she had never claimed in her lifetime. He went on

to say that his father had served the emperor, 'don Carlos'
in Germany, Piedmont and Lombardy, and had fought at
the battle of San Quentin 'close to His Catholic Majesty
don Phelipe'.

It was not a wealth of information, but it was something. It told me that during the years that followed the
disaster at Algiers, Malinche's son had lived the dangerous,
restless life of a European warrior in the forces of the Holy
Roman Emperor. It was a life spent in battle or in readiness
for battle, a life not very different from the one he might
have lived in Mexico had he been born before the Conquest,
instead of one year after it. Except that in Mexico he would
have fought with weapons made of obsidian, rather than
Toledo steel. He would have worn armor made of quilted
cotton rather than metal and, if he proved exceptionally
courageous, a jaguar skin around his shoulders, or eagle
feathers on his head, rather than the red sword-cross of
Santiago on his breast.

Hernán Cortés did not return to Mexico after Algiers. He
stayed on in Spain and tried again and again to win an
audience with Carlos V, but the emperor ignored him.

Cortés's predicament later inspired Voltaire to tell his famous story about those last forgotten years. Voltaire said that one day the old conquistador pushed through the crowds around the emperor's carriage and mounted the steps, but Carlos V did not recognize him and asked who he was. At this Cortés replied sadly, 'One who has given you more kingdoms than you had towns before.' In 1843 when the great blind American scholar, William Prescott, wrote his famous *Conquest of Mexico* for the English-speaking public, he thought this was an apocryphal story. Prescott was probably correct, yet Voltaire's tale captures something of the way the conqueror of Mexico had truly been forgotten in his own country.

After six years lingering around the royal court of Spain, Hernán Cortés finally understood that the emperor would never receive him, and that his grievances against the Crown would never be resolved. He set out for the south, to find a ship to carry him back to Mexico, but in Seville he was overcome by acute stomach pains and dysentery. He must have known he was dying because he called a notary to the house where he was staying, and gave the man instructions for his will.

In the beautiful sixteenth-century reading room of the

Archivo General de Indias, I explored the fifty-eight complex clauses of Cortés's last will and testament with their patrician blend of benevolence and tyranny. Cortés had left strict instructions for the transfer of his bones to Mexico, and their reburial in the same tomb as those of his dead children. He had instructed that fifty poor men should be given woolen capes and tunics and a gold coin each, and asked to carry lighted torches in his funeral possession. He named his many servants and left them various sums of money and orders that they should be given food and lodging, and the wages owed to them. To the younger female servants he left dowries 'to help them marry'.

He ordered hospitals, a monastery and a theological college to be built in Mexico City at the expense of his estate. He left handsome sums of money to his wife, doña Juana, and their three daughters back in Mexico, but he warned that if any of the daughters should marry against the wishes of their mother or their brother, his successor, they would forfeit their inheritance. He left a generous sum to his daughter, Catalina Pizarro, the girl who had been legitimized with Martín and Luis in 1529, and to the mestiza daughter called Leonor whom Isabel Moctezuma had borne him in 1527.

How had Malinche's son fared in his father's will? Eight years earlier Cortés had created an entailment in which he named the younger Martín Cortés, his son by doña Juana, as his heir and successor. But Cortés left a provision that should this boy die, and should his legitimate sisters also die, the estate would pass to his son by Malinche. In his will Cortés confirmed this sequence of succession, but in order to be certain he had provided sufficiently for his 'natural' sons, Martín and Luis, Cortés directed that each of them receive from his estate one thousand gold ducados every year for the rest of their lives.

It was a fabulous endowment, equal to a viceroy's annual salary, but it was not a gift without obligation. In return Cortés commanded 'the said don Martín and don Luys' to serve and obey their younger brother in all the things he proposed, and to treat him honestly as head of the family wherever they went. They were in no way to disobey or fail to serve 'our Lord, his holy religion and Catholic faith, or his natural King' by whom Cortés meant Carlos V and his heir, the prince Felipe. 'And,' he concluded, 'if either of the said don Martín or don Luys commits a disobedience or non-compliance in such a way as to bring shame or notoriety on the family they will lose the benefits bequeathed to them.

Should such disgrace occur,' he warned from beyond the grave, 'I order that they be estranged from my house and my progeny.'

✻

Family and kinship meant everything to Cortés. Yet as he prepared himself for death an ethical question with profoundly universal resonance was also on his mind. 'On the question of the slaves of New Spain taken as ransom in war,' he said in clause number thirty-four of his will, 'there have been many doubts and opinions expressed about whether one can, with good conscience, have them or not. As yet,' he continued, 'the question of what one must do to relieve one's conscience in this matter has still not been determined.'

He was right to say that many doubts and opinions had been expressed on the question of slavery. The Spanish empire never enjoyed the kind of unwavering certainty, the sense of manifest destiny, that epitomized the British empire's later conquests in the Americas, Africa, India and Australia. Among Spaniards, the enslavement of conquered peoples was a subject of tension and debate from the moment Columbus made landfall in Cuba. Queen Isabella herself had obstructed his attempts to make 'her subjects' his slaves. Twenty years later a Dominican priest in the Caribbean, Antonio de Montesinos, had warned his Spanish congregation that they were living and dying in mortal sin because of their tyrannical behavior toward the island's Indigenous people. 'Are they not men?' he had thundered at his parishioners. 'Have they not reasoning minds?'

In 1547, as Cortés lay dying, that other great Dominican, Bartolomé de Las Casas, was still waging his own fierce campaign to protect the people of the Americas. His influence coalesced perfectly with the emperor's determination to limit the wealth and power of the conquistador class. It had led to the promulgation, six years earlier, of the New Laws, las Leyes Nuevas, prohibiting the enslavement of the 'Indians' of the Caribbean and the American mainland.

So what did Cortés mean when he said in his will that the question of what one must do to relieve one's conscience in the matter of slavery had not yet been determined? Ten years earlier, in a royal inquest into the question of slavery, he had argued the case for its necessity. In 1547, as he made his last will and testament, he knew the New Laws had not yet been enacted, and must have hoped they might be amended or withdrawn altogether.

Slavery was not an abstract matter of Christian ethics or

theology for Hernán Cortés, for his wealth and that of his descendants depended on captive Amerindian labor. But now that he was dying he had to deal with this moral quandary, and he did so in the only way he could. He ordered his son and heir to do everything possible to determine the correct approach to the troubling question of slavery. 'I charge don Martín, my son and heir,' he commanded, 'and all who succeed him in my estate, to take all steps to find out what is necessary in order to relieve my conscience and theirs.'

In 1843, when William Prescott wrote *The Conquest of Mexico*, he thought Cortés remarkable for having questioned the morality of a system on which the survival of his dynasty depended. Prescott could not help but see the parallel between the conqueror's ethical quandary and the dilemma only just beginning to concern the United States of America. 'The state of opinion in respect to the great question of slavery in the sixteenth century,' he wrote, 'bears some resemblance to that which exists in our time, when we may hope it is approaching its conclusion.'

The distance in time between our world and that of William Prescott is a mere one hundred and fifty years. So it comes as a shock to realize that at the time he wrote those words, slavery was still legal in his country, and that the battle to abolish it was very new. Prescott was a Yankee from Massachusetts, not a slave-owner from Virginia or North Carolina, yet his beautiful and circuitous nineteenth-century English makes it difficult to pin down precisely how he felt about 'the great question of slavery'. He seemed convinced, however, that abolition was more difficult and far more complex in his own country than it had been in sixteenth-century Mexico.

'There,' he said, 'the seeds of evil, but lately sown, might have been, with comparatively little difficulty, eradicated. Whereas now, they have struck their roots deep into the social system, and cannot be rudely handled without shaking the very foundations of the political fabric. It is easy to conceive,' he continued, 'that a man who admits all the wretchedness of the institution and its wrongs to humanity, may nevertheless hesitate to adopt a remedy, unless he is satisfied that the remedy itself it not worse than the disease. That such a remedy will come with time,' he concluded, 'who can doubt that has confidence in the ultimate prevalence of the right, and the progressive civilization of his species?'

Prescott's fear for his country's political unity, and its

prosperity, was well-founded, given the terrible Civil War to come. He was right to describe Bartolomé de Las Casas and his Dominican colleagues as the abolitionists of their day. But he was mistaken, or perhaps being disingenuous out of loyalty to his own country, when he remarked that in Cortés's time the 'seeds of evil' had only recently been sown. Spain, like all the old Roman countries of the Mediterranean, had a long tradition of slavery, as did pre-Hispanic Mexico, so the 'seeds' of Mexican slavery had been sown in ancient times. That is why the opposition of Las Casas toward such a long-established system and Carlos V's response to the Dominican's enlightened fury seems astonishing in retrospect.

Cortés died the same year Cervantes was born. It is strange yet fitting to think that the life of the man who would immortalize the illusions, and delusions, of conquistadors through his tragic knight *Don Quixote*, should begin with the death of the most famous conquistador of all.

In May I left Seville and went to the nearby village where Cortés had died a month after making his will. I rang the doorbell at the convent in the main street and waited. It was a sultry morning and far below me in the distance

I could see the delta plains of the Guadalquivir, and the river itself winding slowly toward the Atlantic. The village had begun its life as a Roman fortress town, and its name, Castilleja de la Cuesta, little castle on the hill, recalls those ancient beginnings. From up here, I thought, the Roman sentinels could have seen anything that moved for miles around.

A young novice opened the door. I explained why I had come and she invited me inside. We walked together down a shining corridor bordered with the pretty tiles one sees everywhere in Andalucia, and as we walked she explained that the building had been the house of a judge when Cortés came here to die. It had later become a ducal palace and later again a refuge for Irish priests fleeing English persecution until, eventually, it evolved into the convent-school it is today. When we reached the end of the passage I saw a chapel to my right and, beside it, a shady garden. The novice opened a high wooden door on our left.

'We believe this was his room,' she said as she ushered me inside.

It was a spacious chamber with a cool monastic elegance. Its whitewashed walls were bordered with red, blue and black tiles, and two tall windows opened onto the sunlit patio.

In Madrid, in winter, it would be far too cold, but in spring, in Andalucia, it was perfect. There was little furniture: two sixteenth-century wooden chairs, one with a worn red cushion, one black sea-chest, some brass candlesticks and three vases. A bed must once have stood somewhere within this space. It was gone now, but a collection of books on the windowsill gave the curious sense that the room was still inhabited.

On Friday the second of December Cortés had summoned a village notary to this room and gasped out several changes to the will he had made a few weeks earlier in Seville. He had previously ordered that if he should die 'in these kingdoms of Castille' his body should be placed in the parish church of the city or village where he died and later transferred to Mexico. He had not, perhaps, expected to die in such a humble place as Castilleja de la Cuesta, for he now revoked that order and directed instead that his body be placed in the parish church of Seville until it could be taken to Mexico. Next he ordered that money he owed to a man from Jerez be paid to that man's family.

Cortés reminded his heir and successor, the younger Martín Cortés, that he must comply with all his wishes and commands, and he added one final startling clause to his codicil. 'In my said testament,' he said, 'I ordered that don

Luis Cortés, my son, should be paid every year all the days of his life, certain monies from the goods and rents of my estate. I now revoke and annul and give to no-one the said order.' With that he disinherited the boy he had gone to so much trouble and expense to legitimize with Malinche's son in 1529. But why? What can this middle Cortés brother, who is always such a shadowy figure in this family story, have done to inflame his father's anger? The clause lies there in that deathbed codicil, an inexplicable and silent accusation.

Whatever it was that provoked that sudden act of dispossession the scribe wrote down what he was told. At the end of the document he noted that due to the gravity of his illness the marqués [Cortés] was unable to hold a quill, therefore the scribe signed for him in the presence of a Franciscan, Diego Altamirano, and several other men, whose names he also gives in full. Friday the second of December 1547 was the last day of Cortés's life. Later that evening he died.

The novice had waited patiently while I walked the room, examining the furniture, wondering where the bed had stood and thinking about the men, they were all men, who had been with Cortés that night. When she saw that I was finished she asked if I would like to visit the garden I had glimpsed on the way in. We left the room, and I felt a shiver of regret as she closed the door behind us. We walked across the bright patio, past the chapel and down a path that wound through palms and bougainvillea, hibiscus and honeysuckle.

'They say he planted this tree over here,' she said as we walked past a shrine to the Virgin Mary.

'But I think someone must have planted it for him,' she added, 'given that he was so sick when he arrived here.'

We came to the tree.

'It's nearly five hundred years old,' she said looking up into its branches. It was a New World tree — a *Casamira edulis* — of immense height and beauty.

On the bus back to Seville I thought about that list of people who had stayed with the dying Cortés. William Prescott said in his nineteenth-century *Conquest of Mexico* that Cortés was cared for on his deathbed by his son, 'who watched over his dying parent with filial solitude.' Prescott did not say which son, but he knew there were two boys called 'Martín' and it seems clear from the text that he meant doña Juana's child, rather than Malinche's. Yet no 'Martín Cortés' was listed among those present at Castilleja de la Cuesta on the last day of Cortés's life, nor the following day when his will and his codicil were read aloud in public.

If either son had been there his presence would surely have been noted.

※

Artists have a name for the profuse rings of light visible to the human eye only with the aid of a camera obscura. They call them 'circles of confusion'.

Circles of confusion seem to envelop the half-brothers called 'Martín Cortés' in the years following their father's death. Once they returned to Mexico the confusion would clear and Malinche's son would be easily distinguishable from his brother, the marqués, but in Spain I had only a name and a handful of dates to help me identify them. I longed to see them as their contemporaries must have seen them: as brothers who shared a name, but were separated by ten years, by different ranks, and by distinctive racial features, for the younger was the son of a Spanish woman, the older the child of an Amerindian mother.

From the moment Cortés brought his sons together in 1540 they seem to shadow each other through Europe, as if laying traps for anyone seeking to follow their journey through life. Did both sons serve the prince as pageboys? Cortés described Malinche's son, on several occasions, as a page to 'the prince Phelipe', but I never saw him make such a reference to his younger son by doña Juana, and Malinche's son was the only boy whose presence I had seen recorded in the index at the archives of Simancas. Did both boys go to Algiers with their father, or only Malinche's son? Did both or one Martín Cortés take part in the famous battle of St Quentin, between Calais and Paris, in 1555? And did one or both brothers travel to England with the prince the previous year for his marriage to his cousin, Mary Tudor?

In April, at the archives at Simancas, I had asked whether a list existed of the Spaniards who had accompanied the prince to England. 'But everyone in Spain went,' the archivist had responded with a quiet laugh. It was almost true. Felipe's entourage was famous for the number and magnificence of its delegates, and for the thousands of soldiers who escorted them. When the prince sailed from north-west Spain in July 1554 with his first, benevolent armada, his fleet is said to have comprised more than a hundred vessels.

Felipe's biographer, Henry Kamen, says the Spanish visitors to England were elated at first to be in the legendary land of King Arthur. But their stay was not a happy one. English weather dismayed them, and so did the English people, whom they found 'white, pink and quarrelsome'. The

Spaniards were perturbed by English attachment to beer —
'they drink more of it,' one Spanish nobleman observed, 'than
there is water in the river at Valladolid' — and perplexed by
the homely ladies of Mary Tudor's court, because in the
streets outside the palace they saw many beautiful women.

Was Malinche's son among those disappointed Spanish
nobles in England for the royal wedding that year? He must
have been, given that both his father and his own son attested
that he had spent years in the service of the prince. But in
England it is only his twenty-two year old brother for whom
we have a positive sighting. The reference occurs in a chivalric
work entitled *Honor Military and Civill* and printed in
London in 1602. In it the author relates that in December
1554 a joust was organized in the great yard at Westminster
'in knightly homage to the ladies of the court'. It lasted from
midday until five in the afternoon, and among the knights
who tilted for their ladies' favor were Sir Thomas Percy, Sir
George Howard, Prince Philip and 'the Marquis of the Valley,
the son of Hernán Cortés'.

It can look now as if Cortés placed Malinche's son in a
humiliating position by commanding him to serve and obey

his younger brother as head of the family wherever they went. Yet the situation in which the first-born Martín Cortés found himself was not uncommon and, therefore, not implicitly demeaning. Succession was a complex matter among the Spanish nobility, with their blended families full of step-siblings and half-siblings. The chosen son and heir, whether younger or older, was expected to rule his brothers and sisters, and they were expected to follow him as part of his retinue.

Hernán Cortés had been under no obligation to legitimize his first-born son. Martín would have understood the dedication that process had required, and must have felt grateful for the many privileges his father had won for him. Besides, the possibility of succeeding to Cortés's title and estates was not as slight as it might now seem. Mortality was high in sixteenth-century Spain, multiple and rapid deaths within families were common, and it was not unthinkable that an entire line of succession could be wiped out in one epidemic.

But if Cortés did not love Malinche's son any less than his son by doña Juana, as he had declared so passionately in 1532, why did he not name him as his immediate heir and successor? In sixteenth-century Spain there was no legal barrier to the succession of an illegitimate or legitimized son but when Cortés married Juana de Zúñiga he entered a family of great lineage and powerful royal connections. Only a fool would have given a child born of his former concubine precedence over the children of his aristocratic wife, and Cortés was demonstrably not a fool.

The first-born Martín Cortés was twenty-five when his father died, and he would have understood all this. He was a man of the sixteenth century and he would have known that what the dying Cortés wanted was for him to be a loyal member of the noble house he had founded. It may well have been true that Cortés loved his first-born son more than any of his other children. But how happy or unhappy Martín's situation turned out to be would depend to a great extent on his fifteen-year-old brother who was now the second Marqués del Valle and the head of their family.

In 1550 Malinche's son was twenty-eight. According to his own later testimony, he spent that year in Europe, fighting in the armies of the Holy Roman Emperor. Meanwhile his younger brother commissioned a biography of their father, and the man he chose to write it must have seemed a perfect choice for the task.

Francisco López de Gómara had been Cortés's chaplain and his ardent admirer since Algiers. He was also a fine humanist scholar who had trained in Rome. López de Gómara went to work with his quills, his inks and parchments, and by 1552 his book was ready for copying and publication. He called it *La Conquista de México: The Conquest of Mexico* by which he meant the Aztec city, Mexico-Tenochtitlán, rather than the present-day nation of Mexico, which had not yet evolved and would not receive that name for another two centuries.

Spanish readers loved the book, but when it reached the hands of Bernal Diaz del Castillo in Guatemala, he deplored the way López de Gómara had extolled Cortés's courage and genius, as if he alone had conquered Mexico. Diaz del Castillo's resentment is understandable: he had fought and suffered and seen with his own eyes the things this scholarly priest described from the sheltered cloisters of Valladolid. His exasperation was such that he decided then and there to write his own authentic conquistador's account of the Conquest. He would call it *Historia Verdadera de la Conquista de la Nueva España: The True History of the Conquest of New Spain.*

But Bernal Diaz del Castillo was far away in Guatemala on the other side of the Atlantic, and in any case he was a man of little influence. In Spain López de Gómara's book found an infinitely more dangerous enemy in the formidable Dominican, Bartolomé de Las Casas. Las Casas was the avowed enemy of all conquistadors in the Americas. He condemned López de Gómara's admiring portrait of Cortés because he condemned the Conquest itself and all who had taken part in it. He saw the book as an apologia for conquistador crimes against the native peoples of Mexico. 'López de Gómara, a secular priest,' he wrote coldly, '… was never in the Indies, and wrote nothing other than what Cortés told him to write.'

The year after the book's publication, the prince, Felipe, banned it. He offered no reasons for his decision — he had no need to justify his actions in such matters — but can he have listened as Las Casas denounced López de Gómara's book and have acted on what he heard? It seems possible. The Dominican had for years enjoyed the confidence of Felipe and his father Carlos V and, in banning Cortés's biography, Felipe would have been following the tradition established by his great-grandparents, Queen Isabella and King Ferdinand, of extinguishing the pretensions of overly ambitious Spanish nobles. There was also the matter of some elegiac verses the younger Martín Cortés had written and which López de Gómara appended to his final chapter.

'Father, whose fortune this base world inappropriately possessed, *cuya suerte impropriamente … poseía*,' they began, 'whose valor enriched our age, rest now eternally in peace.' There are several possible English translations for that adverb, *impropriamente*. It could mean 'inappropriately', 'undeservedly', 'incorrectly', even 'improperly', but not one of these interpretations is likely to have pleased a royal adviser, or a prince, alert to the long conflict between Hernán Cortés and the Spanish Crown. They could easily be taken to imply that the son who had written them beneath the rather pompous title 'Don Martín Cortés at the Tomb of his Father' shared his father's resentment toward the Spanish Crown.

Whatever it was that inspired the prince's action, his prohibition of Cortés's biography meant that in 1553 the Cortés brothers, Martín and Martín, and the disinherited Luis, were touched for the first time by the shadow of royal disapproval.

The younger Martín Cortés was twenty when the ill-fated book he had commissioned was published. Could he really have been naïve or arrogant enough to think his lines would not cause offence? Perhaps. He would later be renowned for his ability to offend even those who wished him well, and López de Gómara himself seemed to imply a few things about him in his dedication in the book's preface.

'To the very illustrious don Martín Cortés, Marqués del Valle,' he wrote, 'to no-one ... could I dedicate *Historia de la Conquista de México* more appropriately than to your Illustrious Lordship, in the hope that along with your patrimony you may inherit its history.' López de Gómara went on to remind the young marqués that since he had benefited from his father's wealth and fame, he should strive to emulate his father's deeds, 'and to spend well what he has left you.' He seemed particularly concerned that his young patron should manage his inheritance well. 'It is no less praiseworthy or virtuous or arduous to retain one's wealth than to increase it,' he told him, sounding like a prudent aunt from Jane Austen. 'Your Lordship,' he concluded, 'should feel as proud of the deeds of your father as of his wealth, which he won so honorably in a Christian cause.'

What, exactly, was López de Gómara saying here in the very public arena of a best-selling book? Did his concluding sentence suggest he thought his young patron too proud of his father's wealth and not proud enough of his deeds? Could he, as early as 1552, have seen in the second marqués the cupidity and extravagance for which he later became notorious?

One cold autumn morning in October 1556 the Old World of Martín Cortés changed forever. That morning Carlos V rode on horseback through the streets of Brussels with his son, Felipe, by his side. At the royal palace they dismounted and entered its great hall, where the grandest dukes and princes of Europe had gathered to await his arrival.

As a prince aged sixteen Carlos had come to Brussels to accept the throne of Spain. He had now returned to abdicate it. At fifty-five he was exhausted by his life in the saddle, and by the immensity of his imperial role. It had been his fate to wrestle with the audacious Martin Luther and the rising tide of the Reformation, with the genius of his fellow emperor and great enemy, Suleyman the Magnificent, and with the ethical dilemmas posed by Spanish expansion in the Americas. Even the ride through Brussels, the process of dismounting and walking into the palace, must have been physically and mentally painful for him.

The assembled nobles waited in the great hall of the palace as the emperor looked quickly at some scribbled notes in his hand. Then, in a voice filled with emotion, he began to speak, not in his native Flemish, nor in the Spanish he had acquired as a young king, but in French. 'In the course of my expeditions, sometimes to make war, sometimes to make peace, I have been nine times into High Germany, six times into Spain, and seven into Italy,' he said through tears. 'Four times into France, twice into England and twice into Africa … I have crossed the Mediterranean eight times and the Spanish sea twice,' by which he meant the Bay of Biscay, '… and soon I shall make a fourth voyage [to Spain] when I return there to be buried.' He recalled the many battles and wars in which he had fought, and as he did the nobles before him began to weep. He lamented his failure to achieve the peace he said he had always desired for Europe. He told his tearful audience that although he had never willingly trampled on the rights of any man, he begged forgiveness if he had done so.

Apart from his trembling voice the only sounds in the palace were the sighs and sobs of those who had gathered to hear him. They knew they were witnessing a rare event, for Carlos V was the first European emperor to abdicate his many crowns since Diocletian, that other great soldier-emperor, who had relinquished his imperial power twelve hundred years earlier. At the end of Carlos's abdication speech his son, Felipe, knelt before him to receive his blessing. From that moment on he became the ruler of his father's European kingdoms, and of Spain's fledgling empire in the Americas.

The passing of one monarch and the accession of another can inspire profound symbolism among those who witness and remember it. Depending on what occurs later it may come to represent the beginning, or the end, of hope and prosperity. Felipe's accession that morning in Brussels is now understood to have marked the end of the glorious Humanist era of Erasmus and Thomas More, of Dürer and Titian, and the beginning of the Counter Reformation with its multiple repressions. But those gathered in the palace that morning could not have seen the moment in history at which they stood. That kind of understanding can only come later, from a distance and with the passing of time.

Carlos V's Flemish singers and musicians had traveled everywhere with him since he was a youthful prince in Ghent. They had filled every moment of his life with their exquisite harmonies, knowing that he listened with the cultivated ear of a connoisseur. There is no mention of their presence in Brussels that day, but a beautiful song they are known to have performed has often been identified with the emperor's abdication. 'A thousand times I regret to leave you,' goes the 'Emperor's Song'. 'So great is my suffering and painful woe, that my days will soon be ended.'

In the Museo del Prado I had seen the final portrait Titian painted of Carlos V not long before he abdicated. It showed him dressed soberly, although luxuriously, in a dark sable cloak. His eyes still shone with bright intelligence but his face looked pale and gaunt beneath his black velvet hat. It was strange to see him seated instead of standing in masculine assurance with his hunting dog by his side, the way Titian had painted him as a young emperor at the zenith of his imperial power.

Abdication is an uncommon event and never a simple matter to organize. It was another year before Carlos left the Low Countries and arrived on the northern coast of Spain, near present-day Santander. Then this once proud equestrian was carried in a sedan chair through the mountains toward the remote monastery town in Extremadura, where he had chosen to end his days.

He carried with him the many beautiful Titians and Flemish masters I had seen in the Museo del Prado in Madrid. He took the silver-cased organ he liked to play, and the books by Erasmus and Vivas and More and Guevara that had guided him throughout his life, and he also took with him an eleven-year-old boy known to everyone as Gerónimo. The boy was his youngest child. He had been born to a woman in Germany but taken from her to be raised in Spain by the emperor's favorite court musician. His identity as the beloved illegitimate son of Carlos V would be kept secret, even from his half-brother, Felipe, for some years yet.

On my last day in Seville I climbed the beautiful staircase in the Archivo General de Indias once more and registered my name at the front desk. While I waited in the reading room I studied the famous portrait of Pedro de Alvarado on the wall above me. He had fought with Cortés and Bernal Diaz del Castillo during the Conquest of the Aztecs, and had spent his life with an Amerindian noblewoman from Tlaxcala, Luisa de Xicotencatl, who had been given to him prior to the battle for Tenochtitlán. The Aztecs had called him 'Tonatio', the sun. They were right to call him this: the painting showed a man with hair and a beard the color of molten iron; a man from Extremadura who died in

Guatemala, leaving his mestiza daughter by his Tlaxcalan lover as his heir and successor.

The director of the reading room showed me to a desk on the balcony. There was, as always, one more stone to turn, one more name to seek. I entered it in the index and waited. Within seconds a document swam before my eyes on the computer screen. It was a list of prospective passengers requesting permission from the House of Trade, La Casa de Contratación, to embark on a voyage to Mexico. The second entry was the one I was looking for. It referred to the wife of Martín Cortés.

'Doña Bernaldina de Porras, native of the city of Logroño,' I read, 'daughter of Francisco de Porras and doña Maria de Agonallo, his wife, requests permission to travel to New Spain in order to resume married life with don Martyn Cortés, her husband, who is in that land, *que está en aquella tierra*, and to take with her their daughter, doña Ana Cortés, and don Fernando Cortés, natural son of don Martyn Cortés.' So Fernando was living with his step-mother at the time she made her application and may well have been raised by her.

Logroño, where Bernaldina de Porras was born, lay along the ancient route to the shrine of Santiago de

Compostela, in the north-western corner of Spain. As a knight of the Order of Santiago, Martín Cortés would have been obliged to make a pilgrimage to that shrine at least once in his life, and to place a scallop shell in his hat to show that he had done so. Perhaps he was on his way there when he married doña Bernaldina.

I could see no date on the document but I knew Martín Cortés had sailed for Mexico in 1562, so his wife must have made her application some time later. Their separation did not surprise me. Atlantic crossings were difficult and dangerous and it made sense for him to go ahead and prepare the way for her. I noticed that Bernaldina de Porras, like her mother, had been entitled to use the honorific 'doña'. It implied that she was a member of the lesser nobility at least, but her father had not been accorded the masculine equivalent, 'don'. Her name and the suggestion that her parents belonged to different social ranks, that she was born in Logroño and had a daughter called Ana, was as much as I ever learned about the wife of Martín Cortés.

That night I walked slowly along the Guadalquivir. It was a warm, fragrant evening, the jacaranda trees were in flower, and in the darkness below me the current moved slowly toward the Atlantic. 'The river Guadalquivir has beards of garnet, *barbas de granates,*' the poet Federico García Lorca had written. 'The river Guadalquivir winds through orange and olive trees.' In June or July 1562 Martín Cortés had traveled down that watery highway, between those orange and olive trees and beards of garnet, to a ship waiting at the river mouth to carry him back to Mexico. He did not go alone. His younger brother, the marqués, and his disinherited brother, Luis, went with him, and they carried their father's bones with them. The time had come to bury them in Mexico, in accordance with his last wishes.

How did Malinche's son feel as the wind filled the sails of his ship, as he heard the vessel's timbers and its hemp-lines straining, and it moved out into the Atlantic? Was he eager to return to his place of birth, or did he go as a reluctant member of his brother's retinue? Was he apprehensive about the voyage ahead? Twenty years earlier he had survived the shipwreck off Algiers, and as a soldier in the imperial army he must have endured sea travel across the Mediterranean during his forays to Germany and Piedmont and Lombardy. But the journey to Mexico would be an ocean voyage of at least a month's duration, and this time he was leaving the Old World, which was the only world he knew, to return to a New World of which he probably remembered little.

City of Illusion

Mexico

In early October 2001 I followed Martín Cortés back to Mexico, and on the way I paused for some days in Los Angeles. It was a grey dawn when I arrived, and the usually frantic airport felt empty and deserted.

That night my friends in the city of angels showed me some footage they had shot in Mexico a few months earlier. They were preparing a film about Malinche, and in a secluded park not far from where her child was born, they had found a statue of her with Hernán Cortés. It was a study in bronze of the parents of modern Mexico and their son 'the first mestizo'.

I watched as their camera lens moved silently around the figure of Malinche. She looked melancholy and thin, and almost as young as she must have been in real life. She stretched her arm toward us and, as the camera panned slowly back, it revealed the small, carved figure of a boy at her knee. 'Look,' she seemed to say, 'this is my child.' But with his plump face the bronze Martín Cortés looked more like a European cherub than the mestizo boy he was meant to represent.

Suddenly a real child of about eight years old entered the frame. He wore the leather sandals, loose white shirt and cotton pants of a village boy. His black hair was cut with geometric precision above his dark eyes. His skin shone like copper. He climbed swiftly up onto Malinche's knees as if he had done this many times before. He placed his hand in hers and leaned back against her breast to survey the world around him.

'Martín must have looked like him,' my friend whispered.

We watched in silence, scarcely breathing, afraid to disturb his innocent mime, because it suggested with such poignancy the way the real Martín Cortés might once have climbed into his mother's lap. Except of course that by the time he reached this boy's age he was already far away from her at the royal court of Spain.

The ship that carried Martín Cortés back to Mexico limped into the port of San Francisco de Campeche in September

BOY ON STATUE OF MALINCHE IN MEXICO CITY

From the documentary Malinche: The Noble
Slave, *courtesy of Saltillo Films*

1562. Its appearance on the horizon caused consternation in the town: watchmen rang the church bells in alarm; armed guards set out in a frigate to intercept the strange vessel they took for a French or English pirate ship. But as they drew closer they realized it was a Spanish galleon that had lost its flag and part of its sails. They also learned to their amazement that the sons of Hernán Cortés were on board.

The mayor of San Francisco de Campeche, or Campeche

as it is always known these days, wrote to the king, Felipe II, the following year to give an account of the arrival of the Cortés brothers. He said they and their servants had been almost dead with hunger and thirst when they arrived, for their ship's stores had been lost during the journey. It had been a terrible voyage. They had been blown as far south as present-day Colombia, had struggled back north toward Mexico and were making for the gulf port of Veracruz when another storm engulfed them, destroying their sails and one of their masts and making it impossible to continue their journey.

So a tempest had brought Martín Cortés to the remote corner of Mexico where the prelude to his life had begun. I wondered if he understood the connection. He was now forty years old. Did he know that his mother had spent her childhood in slavery among the Mayans of this region? Or that in March 1519, while she was still a young girl, those same Mayans had given her to his father in the aftermath of a great battle? I suspect he did not know, for slavery, and concubinage, were not conditions a proud Spaniard like Cortés is likely to have acknowledged in the mother of his first-born child. The witnesses to Martín Cortés's admission to the Order of Santiago had described her as 'a principal Indian' and this, I imagine, is what he always believed.

The city of Campeche in which Martín Cortés now found himself was not part of New Spain. That name corresponded closely with the region that had once formed the nucleus of the Aztec tributary empire, while Campeche stood in what had always been Mayan territory. The city derived the final part of its beautiful compound name, San Francisco de Campeche, from the Mayan town, Ah Kin Pech, beside which it had been constructed. It would soon become the first walled city in the Americas as it sought to protect its citizens from pirate attack. But in 1562, when Malinche's son arrived there, it was just a fledgling Spanish town hovering apprehensively on the Caribbean coast, at the base of the Yucatán Peninsula.

Martín Cortés left no account of how he felt as his feet touched his native soil for the first time since childhood. But in the streets below Campeche's elegant balconies he would have heard the languages that might have been his had his mother raised him: the Mayan tongue she had spoken as a child in slavery, and Náhuatl, the Aztec tongue that had brought her to his father's attention. It was the language he must have heard in the hours following his birth, and during the two years that he spent in his mother's care.

In Campeche he would have seen, for the first time in his adult life, men and women like himself who were neither

Mayan nor Aztec nor Spanish, but children of Spanish fathers and Amerindian mothers and, in a handful of celebrated cases, of Spanish mothers and Amerindian fathers. They, like him, were children of the Conquest. But whether he identified with them, whether he saw them as fellow members of the same brave new race is impossible to say.

Did a shiver of recognition touch him when mestizo children served him meals on elegant platters in the grand houses where he dined, or when mestizo faces passed him by in the streets of Campeche? Martín Cortés left no record of any such awareness, and even as I asked myself that question I knew he might not have shared my voyeuristic interest in his cultural identity. He had lived a privileged life at the royal court of Spain and must have seemed in every way a Spanish nobleman in his dress, his language and his manners. For all I knew he felt like one, in his loyalties, in his sense of who he was and where he belonged.

At the end of October, on the eve of All Souls, the marqués's wife, Ana, who had been pregnant throughout that terrifying voyage, gave birth to a son called Gerónimo. The infant was not her first child. The first, who was just a few years old, had been left behind in the safer environment of Spain and, like his cousin, the son of the first-born Martín Cortés, he had been named after his paternal grandfather: Fernando Cortés.

Three months after the birth of his nephew, Martín Cortés left Campeche with his brothers. They sailed down the gulf coast toward the port of Veracruz, and this time they reached it without incident. From there they left the lowland heat behind and rode up through the icy mountains of Tlaxcala, following the same lofty trails his parents had taken forty-four years earlier. In his letter to the king, the mayor of Campeche said that by March they were resident in the marquesado properties that the marqués had inherited from their father. So some time in February 1563, Martín Cortés reached the alpine pass between the great snowcapped cones of Popocátepetl and Iztaccíhuatl, and looked down on the former Aztec capital where his life had begun.

He later described himself as a reticent man 'not much given to rejoicings'. But even a reticent man must have taken pleasure in the welcome he and his brothers received as they entered their father's city. A young kinsman he did not yet know watched them come, and said the festivities began with fanfares and a splendid tournament in which three hundred knights in fine livery and polished breastplates raced their horses across the field. That afternoon the knights led a great procession of two thousand mounted Spaniards dressed in black cloaks into the city. The Cortés brothers rode behind them in the place of honor, and the ladies of the city admired them from balconies draped with fine tapestries. When they arrived in the plaza the viceroy came out to greet them, and that night he gave a splendid banquet in their honor.

The kinsman who recorded all this was called Juan Suárez de Peralta. He was twenty-one when he watched the Cortés brothers make their triumphant entrance into their father's city, and he would be a constant and insightful witness to the tragedies to come. 'What I say is true,' he wrote, sounding like the old conquistador-chronicler, Bernal Diaz del Castillo, 'because I was born in the city of Mexico and was present during those things and know them for certain.'

The city of Mexico-Tenochtitlán, with its airy beauty and its dramatic setting beneath the volcanoes, must have astonished Martín Cortés as it did all Europeans who saw it at that time.

A captive English pirate called Robert Tomson had admired it eight years earlier. 'The said Citie of Mexico hath the streets made very broad, and right,' he wrote, 'that a man being in the high place, at the one ende of the street, may see at least a good mile forward.' Another English visitor noted: 'It hath seven streets in length and seven in breadth with rivers running throw every second street, by which they bring their provisions in canoas.' Its careful, rectilinear design and sense of spaciousness enchanted visitors, for it was nothing like the claustrophobic labyrinths they knew in contemporary Europe. This great New World metropolis had been reconstructed, on its conqueror's insistence, in accordance with its original Aztec design.

Richard Sennett tells us in *Flesh and Stone: The Body and the City in Western Civilization* that by the Middle Ages even those European cities originally designed according to the orderly template of the Romans had fallen into chaos. 'Neither King nor Bishop nor Bourgeois had an image of how the city should look,' Sennett writes. Yet in 1522, amid the ruins of the fallen Aztec capital, Hernán Cortés, who was neither king nor bishop nor bourgeois, had an image of how he wanted his new metropolis to look. He had seen Tenochtitlán in all its glory while it was still an elegant and well-ordered Aztec city. He had resided there for eight months as a guest of the emperor Moctezuma, and the attention he paid to its essential geometry during that time is clear from his letters to Carlos V.

'This great city is built on the salt lake,' he wrote. 'There are four artificial causeways leading to it and each is as wide as two cavalry lances … the main streets are very wide and very straight … all the streets have openings in places so that the water may pass from one canal to another. Over these openings are bridges made of long and wide beams joined together very firmly and so well-made that on some of then ten horsemen may ride abreast.'

Cortés had not wanted to destroy the city, but the Aztecs' refusal to surrender had so confounded and perplexed him that in desperation he had decided to incinerate the royal residences 'so big that a prince with more than six hundred people in his household might be housed in them.' He had hoped the sight of those burning palaces, so emblematic of past magnificence, would force the Aztecs to surrender, but it did not. At the height of battle his interpreter, Martín Cortés's mother, had called to the Aztec jaguar and eagle knights on their temple platforms, urging them to give up, but they had shouted back to her, saying they would never surrender, that even when only one of them remained he would die fighting. They swore, she told Cortés, that they would burn or throw into the water all that they possessed so that he would never have it.

It is clear from Cortés's letter to Carlos V that in the end his conquest of their city was a Pyrrhic victory; that his dismay at having to destroy this jewel of the Americas rather than capture it intact as a symbol of his own vainglory was genuine. But as he stood in the ruins of Tenochtitlán, its vanished beauty still shimmering in his memory, he was inspired to turn away from the labyrinthine alleys he had known in Spain, and try to recover something of the Aztec city he had known and lost.

Martín Cortés had been born around the time it's resurrection had commenced. He was a new child for the New World of post-Conquest Mexico, and when he returned as a grown man forty years later the city had fulfilled his father's dreams. Its streets were indeed wide and straight, its canals had been cleared, and the aqueducts destroyed during the Conquest were once again bringing clean fresh water into the city from the woods of Chapultepec.

In 1972, when George Kubler wrote his famous *Mexican Colonial Architecture of the Sixteenth Century*, he remarked that

Mexico had been colonized during a decade of humanist ascendancy in Spain, whereas Peru was conquered during a decade of anti-humanist reaction. These profoundly different philosophical orientations meant that the post-Conquest city of Mexico flourished in a way Lima never did. In Mexico City the first viceroy and the first archbishop had established a printing shop in which grammars and dictionaries and theological works in Náhuatl, Mayan, Otomi, Totonac and other Amerindian languages were produced. A university with faculties in those languages, as well as medicine, law and theology, had been founded. There were hospitals, schools and convents and, at a safe distance from the city, a judge called Vasco de Quiroga, who was an admirer of Thomas More, had established a utopian community for Aztec families.

Several thousand Spanish residents lived within the straight wide streets and graceful plazas of the post-Conquest city. Free and enslaved Africans lived and worked beside them, but the Aztec survivors of the siege of 1521 lived outside the Spanish sector. Theirs was not an apartheid-style exclusion forced on them by their conquerors. It was a separation they preferred as they struggled to retain their traditional social structure, and survive the epidemics now sweeping their city. In the forty years since their city fell to the

Spaniards its Amerindian residents had been devastated by the disease they called *hueyzahuatl*, 'great sickness', with its disfiguring pustules and its burning fevers, as well as by other European ills they had never before encountered, like chicken pox, measles and influenza. In 1563, when Martín Cortés arrived, they were only fifty years away from the moment at which they might have ceased to exist altogether if their emergent immunological resilience had not suddenly begun to pull them back from the brink of extinction.

But nothing was simple in the post-Conquest city. It was not a bipolar world in which only two possibilities — white or copper-skinned — existed. Nor was it divided purely along racial lines, for class seems often to have prevailed over race as a social marker. Within the Spanish quarter, alongside the most respected members of Spanish society, lived a privileged Indigenous elite that included the Moctezuma family and other nobles. They still spoke their refined and eloquent Náhuatl, but they also now acquired Spanish and Latin. They maintained the old exclusivity from Aztec commoners they had demanded before the Conquest, and they held to the pre-Conquest sumptuary laws that had permitted them, and them alone, to dress in rich and elaborate garments. Except that now they added

Spanish garments to their costume, and married their sons
and daughters to the sons and daughters of the Spanish
viceroy and his aristocratic relatives, rather than to fellow
members of the Aztec nobility.

What was Martín Cortés's place in this complex
phoenix of a city? As the son of the Amerindian concubine
of its Spanish conqueror he was technically a man of mixed
race, a mestizo. But as a privileged child educated at the
royal court of Spain, and the brother of the second Marqués
del Valle, he belonged to the highest echelons of vice-regal
society. Any shame that might have been associated with his
illegitimate birth seems to have been assuaged by his
illustrious family name. If his racial identity mattered to
those around him, their concerns are not explicit in the
documents surviving from that time.

I saw him referred to often as the 'natural' son of Hernán
Cortés, but never as the 'mestizo' son. His racial identity
simply didn't seem to matter. Or else he had been incorporated so fully into the world of Spain—in his dress, his manners,
his demeanor, his disposition — that it went unnoticed.
I began to sense that 'the first mestizo' might not have been
regarded as mestizo in his own time, that his symbolic identity
was more apparent in retrospect than in his own time.

One afternoon, however, sorting through copies of some letters from the second marqués, I came upon a comment he had made about mestizos in general and flinched to think what his words might have meant for Malinche's son. In October 1563 the marqués had written to the king, Felipe II, telling him that he had now been in New Spain for a year and had a number of proposals for its better governance. He recommended, for example, that higher tribute levels be extracted from the Indians. How was it, he asked, that there were so many of them, yet they paid so little to the Crown? He lamented the number of poor Spaniards arriving constantly from Spain and Cuba with no place to live and nothing to eat, and urged the king to do something about these vagabonds. But worse, he told Felipe, were the vast numbers of mestizos, so many that they covered the land. They were born with naturally evil inclinations, he said, *estos naturalmente nacen mal inclinados*, and did great harm to the Indigenous people.

The marqués's opinions were familiar to me. Similar views about the children of Aboriginal women and European men had often been voiced in Australia. 'The mongrel half-caste inherits only the vices of civilization ...' a Northern Territory constable had written in 1896. 'If it is a male he is born for the gallows ... if a female she becomes a wanton devoid of shame.' Had the second marqués seen the mestizo brother who shared his name in that light: as a man born with naturally evil inclinations? Or did he exempt him from his prejudices, the way people sometimes exempt selected friends and family? Either way if these were views the marqués had expounded in his brother's hearing, as well as in his letters to the king, they must have affected the way Martín Cortés thought about himself.

October mornings in Mexico City are bright and cold. Wrapped in a woolen shawl I crossed the plaza they call the 'Zócalo'. I passed the street-sweepers and the early worshippers entering the cathedral, and spoke for a few moments to a guide I knew at the Great Temple of the Aztecs. We talked for a while, and then I took a bus east along Justo Sierra toward the Archivo General de la Nación.

It was still early when I began examining the index for the Cortés family papers in search of anything with meaning for Martín Cortés. I had told myself I would be grateful for a business letter, an account, even the merest receipt. Nothing would be too trivial for my purposes. As I expected, the index was full of his brother, the marqués, and the endless legal battles that had afflicted the lands in the great marquesado he had inherited from his father.

The Indigenous communities of Coyoacán, Cuernavaca, Chapultepec, Tacuba, Zimatlán, Ocotlán, Huastepec and Amilpas had all brought actions against the marqués. In Spanish and Náhuatl, sometimes in iconographic form on the traditional *amatl* paper they had used for centuries, they had complained that he and his father, Hernán Cortés, had exacted excessive tribute from them. The communities had demanded compensation for the lands, the temples and palaces they had lost during the Conquest, and many of them had won their cases either wholly or in part.

I found it strangely disquieting, that morning in the archives, to see that Indigenous Mexicans in the sixteenth century had used the Spanish legal system so effectively against their Spanish conquerors. Where I come from, Indigenous people seeking to recover their lands through the courts are told more often than not, even now, that the tide of history has washed their claims away.

Entry after entry in the index revealed that the marqués had been plagued by litigation from within his family as well as from without. His mother, Juana de Zúñiga, had brought several claims against him over property and money. So had his uncle, and his sisters, and even Juan Altamirano, the man who had raised the young Martín Cortés in his household. Altamirano had accused the marqués of neglecting the financial obligations his father had entrusted to him.

I had almost reached the end of the 1550s, and was becoming disheartened at the absence of Malinche's child, when I came to a long and detailed entry. 'Claim brought by don Martín Cortés, son of don Hernando Cortés, first Marqués del Valle,' it said, 'against don Martín Cortés, his brother and heir to the estate.' I read the passage through once more, my heart pounding. Then I went to gallery four and lodged my request. While I waited for the documents to be retrieved, I paced the room, thinking of the countless mishaps that can befall such old papers, so many that it often seems miraculous that any have survived at all. I need not have worried. Before long the archivist emerged from the shadows of the gallery with a large bundle of parchments.

'Here they are, *Maestra*,' he said, and he handed them across to me.

The story they told was this. In 1557, when Martín Cortés was thirty-five years old and still in Spain, a lawyer had initiated an action on his behalf to recover from his brother, the second marqués, certain mines and slaves granted to him by his father eighteen years earlier.

In neat meticulous letters, in brown ink on vellum, the attorney had explained to the courts that this endowment was meant to be shared between Martín Cortés and his brothers, the second marqués, and Luis Cortés, but that he had as yet derived no benefit from it. For this reason Martín Cortés now asked that his share be transferred to him in full. He no longer wished to be in communion with his brother, his lawyer said, *no quiere estar más en comunión con su hermano*. It seemed an interesting way to express it. Was it merely a legal expression, or something more?

Like all such battles this one had been fought out between lawyers. A certain Juan de Salazar had acted for Martín Cortés. Antonio Ruíz had acted for the marqués. I began working through the parchments, examining each one carefully. 'I, Juan de Salazar, on behalf of don Martín Cortés,' I read again and again, or 'I, Antonio Ruíz, on behalf of don Martín Cortés, second Marqués del Valle ...' But when I came to the thirty-seventh parchment I noticed it began differently. 'I, don Martín Cortés ...' it announced. I leaned forward in my chair. It seemed I was about to hear

Malinche's son speak directly for himself rather than through his lawyer.

It was a power of attorney couched in the typical legal jargon of the sixteenth century. 'Know all you present at the signing of this instrument,' he said, 'that I, don Martín Cortés, being in the town of Berlanga, grant and give through this letter my full, free, complete and abundant power to you señor don Luis de Quesada, my brother-in-law, being in the Indies of New Spain, so that for me, and in my name, you may demand, receive and collect the one thousand ducados due to me each year from the estate of the Marqués del Valle, my brother.' So his half-brother had failed to honor the commands their father had made in his will ten years earlier.

It was not a personal letter to his wife, or son, or daughter, but it was something he had initiated, something he had touched. A professional scribe had written the text, for no man of Martín Cortés's rank would have condescended to write it himself. However, on the third and final page I came to his signature.

His letters sloped evenly toward the right. They were well shaped and clear, and he had employed the conventional elisions of his time, writing 'do' for 'don' and

'Myn' for 'Martyn'. He had drawn a line beneath his name with a firm stroke of ink and had framed it with two elongated figures of eight. It was not a garish signature; he had signed with the confident and graceful hand of a man raised and educated at the royal court, a man who had no need for ostentatious flourish.

I ran my fingers across his name, imagining the way his hand had held the quill that made those letters. What had he been doing in Berlanga? Earlier that year, as I traveled north from Andalucia to Extremadura, I had seen the name 'Berlanga' on the map I carried with me. It was up there in the dark hills of the Sierra Morena, among the old hilltop castles and fortresses along the ancient border between the old Roman provinces of Baetica and Lusitania. I had passed it by without knowing that Martín Cortés had once lived there.

I looked out into the atrium, at the guards standing quietly on its polished floor, at the soft light filtering down on them from the ceiling dome above. If I had understood correctly, Martín Cortés had appointed Luis de Quesada, his brother-in-law, to act for him in Mexico. That was what I thought the document said, but I am never entirely sure of my paleographic skills, and wanted confirmation. In the offices on the other side of the atrium was a scholar who had

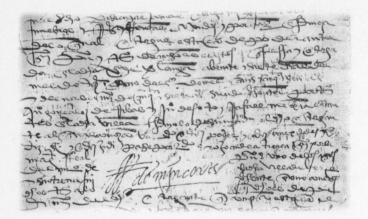

FRAGMENT OF MANUSCRIPT FOR MARTÍN CORTÉS'S
POWER OF ATTORNEY
Archivo General de la Nación

helped me in the past. I decided I would go to her and ask
if she could verify the name for me.

'It was his brother-in-law,' she told me later that day.

She pointed to the words as she read them aloud to me.
'Don Luis de Quesada, my brother-in-law, being in the
Indies of New Spain …'

'Does that help?' she asked.

'It's what I hoped it said,' I replied.

Martín Cortés had six half-sisters in Mexico. Three of
them were daughters of Juana de Zúñiga, who lived with

their mother in the palace Cortés had built for them outside the city, in the town of Cuernavaca. Catalina Pizarro, the girl who had been legitimized with Martín in 1529, resided in the palace with them. Another half-sister, Leonor Moctezuma, the granddaughter of the Aztec emperor, had gone to live in the north with her wealthy Spanish husband. Those five sisters were children of Cortés by his wife and two of his lovers. But Martín's sixth half-sister was Malinche's daughter. She had been born in 1526, during the expedition to Honduras. Her name was Maria Xaramillo, and Luis de Quesada was her husband.

I knew enough about Luis de Quesada to guess how he and Martín Cortés might have come to know each other. Quesada was a member of the aristocratic Mendoza family. He sometimes called himself Luis López de Mendoça in an allusion to that connection. He had married Maria Xaramillo in 1542 when she was sixteen, and in 1555, according to his own *probanza*, or proof of service to the Crown, he had accompanied the prince, Felipe, to England for his marriage to Mary Tudor. That, I suspected, was where he encountered his brother-in-law, Martín Cortés for the first time.

I had often wondered whether Malinche's children had been aware of each other's existence. I thought I might never know for certain. Yet Martín Cortés's power of attorney revealed that they had known about each other and were in contact at least six years before he returned to Mexico. The far-reaching powers he had granted to his sister's husband suggested that a deep sense of trust had existed between them.

It took me two days to read the many parchments contained within that weighty bundle. I learned from them that for five years Martín Cortés had argued firmly, and repeatedly, that his brother, the marqués, was withholding from him what was rightfully his.

The marqués, for his part, had claimed that their father's supposed grant of mines and slaves was not authentic because it lacked the signature of a royal notary. He also argued that the slaves in question had cost him more in food and clothing and medicines than they had produced in silver, and that he alone had borne those costs. He said his father had supported his half-brother, don Martín, during his lifetime, providing him with abundant weapons and horses and servants and everything he needed, and had also paid the many debts Malinche's son had amassed in Spain. Since their father's death, the marqués added, he had continued to support don Martín, his *hermano de suerte*, his 'brother by chance', to such a generous extent that any debt to him would easily have been extinguished by now. The marqués described himself as a generous brother who had been much put-upon by his older sibling. Martín Cortés, for his part, asked only that he should receive what was rightfully his. Which one was telling the truth?

It was a Friday when I finished reading the documents. I left them on my lectern and walked out through the atrium into the garden. Rain clouds were gathering overhead. A hummingbird was drinking from the flowers of a crimson penstamon. Otherwise I was alone. An hour earlier I had learned that the judges had believed Malinche's son, and found in his favor. But while he had been arguing with his brother, the marqués, over the human property their father had left them, an event entirely out of his control had taken place. The New Laws ordering all Indigenous slaves in New Spain to be freed had begun to take effect. It meant that Martín Cortés had spent years fighting for something over which he now had no claim. He had won his share of mines, but would be obliged to pay something at least to his former slaves to work them, or else he would have to purchase African slaves, for their enslavement was still legal. So after all those bitter allegations of greed and duplicity and profligacy, he still had no way of escaping from his life as a member of his brother's retinue.

Later that afternoon, after the rain had stopped, I walked home from the archives, along the crowded market streets toward the plaza and the Great Temple of the Aztecs. The guide I knew was waiting by the ticket office. He had no clients for the moment so we talked about Martín Cortés and I told him how hard Malinche's son had fought to win his share of Indian slaves from his brother.

'Must have been his Spanish blood that made him do it,' he sighed. 'They were the ones who brought slavery to Mexico.'

I understood his disappointment. I had felt it too. But I had seen Moctezuma's tribute list, and knew the Aztecs, like the Mayans, had made slaves of their fellow Amerindians long before the coming of the Spanish. Martín's mother had been just such a slave, so her son's desire to be a slave-owner was as compatible with her Amerindian world as it was with the European world in which he had been raised.

I suspected he never knew about his mother's childhood

in slavery but if he had known, could that knowledge have stirred an unexpected empathy in him toward the men and women he wanted to own? The proposition sounds absurd now, yet after the Conquest several of Hernán Cortés former conquistador companions had repented of their deeds, relinquished their slaves and their hard-won wealth, and joined the Franciscans. Even the great Dominican, Bartolomé de Las Casas, had been a slave-owner in his youth before he became the slavers' greatest enemy. Such epiphanies, such sudden swings of heart and mind, were possible in the world inhabited by Martín Cortés.

Rebellion

The road from Mexico City to Cuernavaca winds slowly down beneath the glittering white cone of Popocatépetl and straight into the heart of what were once the great estates of the Cortés marquesado. One icy Saturday morning I took that road and, at the top of the sierra, in sight of the volcano, I paused to look back at the great smoky city spread out before me.

It was still early and, as always when I see the Valley of Mexico from above, I remembered the generations of hunter-gatherers, like the Aztecs, who had found a home within its fertile basin. The valley drew them in. It beguiled them with its lake water and its rich volcanic soil, and turned them into gardeners and city-builders. On the other side of the sierra, in what is now the state of Morelos, Hernán

Cortés had found his own conquistador paradise. He had filled its warm valleys with silkworms and cherry orchards and vast sugar haciendas. In earlier times its people had paid regular tribute of amaranth, corn, tomatoes, avocados, chocolate and turkeys to their Aztec overlords. Cortés saw no need to abolish such a useful structure. Instead, in the aftermath of the Conquest, he directed the villagers to pay him their precious tribute. He then sold it on at great profit to his fellow conquistadors to form the basis of his new wealth.

But these were the towns and villages the Spanish Crown had taken from him while he was away in Honduras, on the grounds that he had no claim to them. They were the ones they returned to him as part of his new marquesado when he made his conciliatory pilgrimage to Spain in 1528. No sooner had he retrieved them from the Crown than the Indigenous communities commenced their lawsuits against him. In several instances the Crown, alert to Cortés's lordly pretensions, found in the traditional owners' favor and ordered him to lower tribute levels and return several parcels of land to them. So the marquésado was always an uncertain Eden for Hernán Cortés, and twenty years after his death his son and heir was fated to lose it once more.

At the foot of the sierra I took a narrow road through cornfields and palm trees toward the village of Xochitepec. In a Crown Census of 1532, the year his legitimate son was born, Cortés had listed it as part of his marquésado. He spelled it 'Sochitepeque' but however it is written it means 'Place of Flowers' in Náhuatl, and within the village is another village in the form of an old sugar hacienda. Earlier that week my closest friend in Mexico City had told me she believed it once belonged to Martín Cortés. Which Martín Cortés? I had asked her. She said she thought it was the son of Cortés and La Malinche. That was what she had heard. In any case I was curious to see what was said to be a beautiful remnant of the marquesado.

By the time I arrived there, the sun had begun to warm me. A high stone aqueduct ran along beside the plaza and disappeared behind the hacienda walls. I could hear water flowing through it, and when I asked a child eating watermelon where the water originated she told me it came from a natural spring not far away called La Esquina Dorada, the Golden Corner. The aqueduct was very old, she said. It had carried clean water to the village for centuries. I knocked on the immense wooden doors in the walls of the hacienda, and waited. I heard voices from the other side, and after some minutes a young man opened a small aperture to my right. He had been expecting me. My friend in Mexico City had called ahead to ask if I could come.

I stepped through the entrance and we followed the aqueduct's path as it meandered through shade trees and shrines hung with bougainvillea and hibiscus toward the old sugar refinery at the heart of the estate. The hacienda had become a favorite setting for society weddings, and the refinery was now a wedding chapel. Its flagstones shone, its air was cool and fragrant. Huge urns of the white calla lilies Diego Rivera loved to paint filled the alcoves where the furnaces had once stood. It was truly a place of flowers.

There was no sense of the fires that had once burned in the refinery furnaces, or of the sweating, aching bodies of the slaves who had stoked them. Their African names are lost to us, but their Spanish names have survived in the marquesado records. Most had been born in West Africa. Hernando, 'about fifty years old a little more or less', was a native of Mandinga. Juan, Juan Segundo, Manuel, Diego and Nicolás came from 'Biafara', Luis and Pedro from Manicongo, while Marcos and Andrés had come from Mozambique on the eastern side of the continent. Several African women were also listed in the records. Their Spanish names were Ana, Francisca, Marta, Leonor and Maria. The records note that most of them had young children with them.

My guide led me through the cool, cavernous cellars beneath the refinery into a large tranquil courtyard beneath the hacienda residence.

'I can take you upstairs, to the balcony,' he told me, 'but the bedchambers are locked these days.'

He spoke apologetically, but I assured him I was grateful for the merest glimpse of this old hacienda world. We climbed the stairs, and from the balcony I looked out toward the walls of the estate. It had been early when I arrived. Now the sun was high above the trees, and village children sat playing in the shade below.

I followed my guide back down the stairs, and in the courtyard we paused beside a window beneath the balcony that I hadn't noticed on the way up. It opened onto a large and shadowy room. I peered inside and as my eyes adjusted to the dark interior I saw a low, narrow bed. A crucifix hung on the wall above the bed, a sword lay across it, and a collection of other swords and knives had been set out on a wooden table near the door, as if they had just been cleaned. The room looked as if someone still lived in it, someone who took great care with his weapons, someone always on his guard.

Water troughs for horses were still in place around the patio. Which of the brothers called Martín Cortés had once come cantering across its flagstones? One or both? The hacienda's owners in Mexico City believed this beautiful property had once belonged to Malinche's son. But I had found no evidence for his ownership in the archives, and when I asked my guide whether he knew Hernán Cortés had two sons called 'Martín', he was surprised and said he hadn't known. His innocence made me wonder whether that absurd duplication of names in the Cortés family might have caused the usual confusion.

Later that day I took the road to Cuernavaca. The Palacio de Cortés was crowded, as it always is on Sundays, but in the small gallery dedicated to the Cortés family I found the bust of doña Juana I remembered from an earlier visit. It sat poised on an elaborate jewel chest that had belonged to her when she lived within the palace walls. Her hair was pulled back from her face, her hands were pressed together in prayer, and someone had dressed her alabaster likeness in an ancient yellowing blouse that must once have been hers. High up on the wall beside her was the painting I had come to see. It was her son, the second marqués.

I stood on my toes and peered up at him. He had a long and pale face. His nose was thin and narrow and he looked down at me from beneath hooded lids. For his sitting he had chosen a rich blue doublet with extravagant sleeves, a high ruffled collar and frills at the wrist. He wore a sweeping, ivory feather in his broad-brimmed hat and a crimson cloak over his shoulders. His costume looked a gaudy affair compared with the plain black garments his father had preferred. He clasped the pommel of a large sword in his small white hand, but the sword seemed more the typical accoutrement of formal portraiture than a serious weapon, and he looked more like a popinjay than a conquistador.

I thought I detected a similar air of piety in the expressions he and his mother had adopted for their portraits, and I saw a likeness in the ghostly whiteness of their skin. I wished I could have seen a portrait of Malinche's son. If I could have looked into his face would I have found some family resemblance to his brother? Perhaps. But not that pallor, nor those colorless eyes. I felt sure that, like the boy on Malinche's statue, like the men and women I saw each day in

Martín Cortés, the Second Marqués del Valle
Museo de Cuauhnahuac, Cuernavaca, Mexico

Mexico City, the first mestizo's looks had owed more to ancient America than to Europe.

※

The catastrophe that engulfed Malinche's son in 1566 looks now as if it erupted out of nowhere, but I had been following his path toward it all this time, and knew its prelude had begun long before he returned to the land of his birth.

In Mexico the second viceroy had enacted the New Laws prohibiting slavery with greater caution than his counterpart in Peru, who had been murdered by Spanish settlers for his trouble. But when the viceroy of Mexico did enact them, he incurred the bitter wrath of the conquistador class who could now no longer profit from the unpaid labor of their Indian captives. Those who could afford to turned instead to African slavery, but by the time Martín Cortés returned to Mexico that too was being questioned. In 1560 the archbishop of Mexico City had written to Felipe II saying that he could not see why Africans should be made captives any more than Indians. 'May it please our Lord,' he had implored the king, 'that this enslavement cease.'

Soon after, word came of yet another proclamation from the king. Felipe had confirmed his dead father's ruling that lands won in the Americas could not be held in perpetuity by their conquerors, but must revert to the Crown after the second generation. That is why the exasperated conquistador sons of Mexico City rejoiced at the return of the marqués, because they saw him as a natural leader in their battle against a Crown determined to limit their wealth and their power.

They welcomed him as if he were a prince returning to claim his throne and, in a way, that is precisely what the marqués was, for at thirty he possessed both riches and enormous prestige in the vice-royalty. But his admirers had forgotten that he was already blessed with the perpetual inheritance rights for which they longed; and that his prosperity, and that of his descendants, was guaranteed for centuries to come. If they had not been so blinded by his famous name, his noble title and his wealth, they might have realized that, although he enjoyed their adulation, he had no real stake in their battle with the Crown. If they had, the bloodshed to come, and the ordeal of Martín Cortés, might have been avoided.

The young kinsman called Juan Suárez de Peralta who had watched the Cortés brothers enter the city, recorded everything that happened with sorrow rather than Schadenfreude. He said that after the marqués returned to Mexico City his friends among the dashing young conquistador sons could think of nothing but the fiestas and galas and masked balls to which he was devoted. Somewhere in Europe the marqués had learned a Russian custom that he now introduced to them. He would order jugs of wine to be brought to the table and challenge his companions to see who could drink the most. Once the wagers were fixed and the goblets filled, the marqués and his friends would take turns to pour the contents down their throats. Whoever consumed the most without collapsing was declared the hero.

Suárez de Peralta said that on most occasions every man present would eventually crash to the floor in an avalanche of jugs, goblets, candlesticks and vomit. He called the game a 'vice'. It was also an expensive vice, one the marqués could afford because he was exceedingly rich, but one which most of his companions could not. Many of them were obliged to take loans and mortgages to finance their carousing, and Suárez de Peralta said that many families were ruined forever by the few dissolute years their sons had spent as members of the marqués's circle.

He recalled that people outside that fashionable coterie began to resent the way the marqués addressed them with the familiar *vos* instead of the more respectful *vuestra merced*. They were dismayed when he unleashed a lawsuit against a cousin of his who had treated him generously, and scandalized when he began to claim the higher rank of duke and had a lance-page walk before him, carrying a banner adorned with his father's coat of arms. To them the marqués seemed to be usurping the viceroy's role by offering formal receptions and lavish hospitality to visiting Crown bureaucrats, and by adopting a large silver seal with a suspiciously regal coronet above the Cortés insignia for use on his documents.

These incidents seem now like nothing more than clumsy lapses in etiquette, but little by little they began to suggest to the vice-regal authorities that the marqués had rebellion on his mind. It didn't help that the leader of the Peruvian uprising had been a Pizarro kinsman of the Cortés family. Nor did it help that by the time the viceroy informed the royal court in Spain of the marqués's many breaches of protocol, his arrogance and his imperious manners had left him with few defenders in Mexico City. 'Everyone started to criticize the marqués,' Suárez de Peralta remembered later, 'and many swore they could not tolerate him, and all the love and goodwill they had once borne toward him began to disappear because of his conduct.'

There was something else about that vexatious silver seal — something quite aside from the peril into which it led the marqués and his brother. Juan Suárez de Peralta said that inscribed in Latin on its shining face were the words *Martínus*

Cortésus primus hujus nominis Dux Marchio Secundus: Martín Cortés, first son of that name, second marqués. But the marqués was not the first son called Martín Cortés, as he well knew. He possessed every material thing he could ever want in life yet he seemed determined to claim his half-brother's place in the family as well.

Malinche's son said later that although he lived in the marqués's house on the western side of the plaza, he took no part in his brother's merrymaking but would withdraw to his own rooms at such times. So it seems he had no appetite for festivities. Once his wife and children joined him he had them for company. And he had his sister, for he must have met her soon after he returned to Mexico.

How did Malinche's children greet each other? Maria Xaramillo de Quesada lived just a few blocks from the plaza, at what is now the corner of Minas and Lazaro Cárdenas. Her house is gone now, but I imagine a recognition scene within its walls, like that in Shakespeare's many tales of brothers and sisters, parents and children, reunited after shipwreck and war and family intrigue has torn them apart. 'Thrice-welcome, drowned Viola! My father had a mole upon his brow.'

Whatever intimate conversations this long-separated brother and sister shared were not recorded and belong only to them. They must have spoken about their mother, yet Martín had spent only two years with her, and Maria not much more, for in 1547 she had testified that her father had then been married to his second wife for twenty years. Maria had been born in 1526 so if she was correct in her time frame, even if she were out by a year or two, she would have been very young when her mother died.

Even if Malinche's children did not recall much about her, they could have gathered information from old conquistadors and servants who had known her. But Martín Cortés and his sister were not the only people in Mexico City to remember their mother, and not the only ones to invoke her name. In 1565 the second marqués began an affair with a certain lady also known as 'doña Marina' and, in response, some anonymous wit composed a snide and prescient little poem that was soon being whispered throughout the city. 'Through Marina, I'm a witness,' it ran, 'that a good man won this land. And through a woman of the same name, I swear it will be lost.'

The writer, Richard Rodriguez, describes Mexico City as the play that Shakespeare did not write. 'Now the great city swells under the moon,' Rodriguez says, 'seems, now, to breathe of itself … a Globe, kind Will, not of your devising, not under your control.' Within that globe lies the immense plaza in which, and around which, the tragedy of the brothers called Martín Cortés began to unfold early in 1566.

In March that year a rich and fashionable young man named Alonso de Avila organized a masquerade to celebrate the birth of twins to the marqués and his wife. Juan Suárez de Peralta said that Avila was a favorite of the marqués, and 'one of the most splendid knights in Mexico City, *era de los más lúcidos caballeros que había en Mexico*.' Suárez de Peralta praised Avila's charming manners, his elegant clothes, his complexion 'as fair as a lady's'.

Alonso de Avila's masquerade was a reenactment of the Conquest forty years earlier, in which his father had taken part at Hernán Cortés's side. Avila led a procession of his friends and servants into the plaza. All of them were dressed as Aztecs, and he appeared as Moctezuma, although later he changed into his father's old conquistador armor and assumed the role of Cortés. They rode into the plaza and up to the marqués's house. When the marqués and his wife

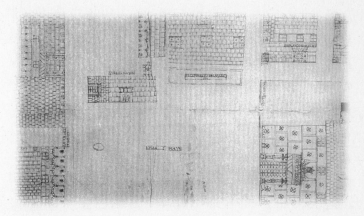

PLAN OF THE CENTRAL PLAZA, MEXICO CITY, 1563
Archivo General de Indias

appeared in their grand doorway, Avila's 'Aztecs' presented them with bouquets and coronets of roses. '*Suchiles*', they called them, for they had adopted the Náhuatl word *xochitl* for flower.

According to later testimony someone called to the marquesa, telling her to take the crown she was offered. Another witness would remember that among the paper messages offered to the marqués with a floral crown was a little rhyme telling him not to fear the fall for he would rise to greater heights. '*No temas la caida*,' it advised him, '*pues es para mayor subida.'* Later that evening, during the banquet that followed, Alonso de Avila knelt before the marqués and presented him with a set of jugs and drinking vessels inscribed with a crown and, beneath each crown, the letter 'R' for *rey*, or king.

There is something slightly mad and deeply portentous about Alonso de Avila's masquerade. It took place at the height of that long period of provocative conduct on the part of the marqués, and in the perilous context of recent conquistador rebellions in Peru and Nicaragua. The masquerade became a disaster for all who took part in it, for soon after, perhaps that same evening or early the following day, one of the guests left the mansion where the marqués and his friends had been cele-brating, walked the short distance across the plaza to the royal houses, and told the authorities what he had seen. The judges of the royal council listened to what he said, and were con-vinced that a conspiracy against the Crown, led by the Marqués del Valle and his brothers, was afoot in Mexico City.

Where was Martín Cortés during the masquerade? If he was as reserved as he later claimed, he probably took no part in it and certainly his participation was not noted in the formal

Crown investigation that began soon after. Yet the masquerade was the beginning of the end for him.

Juan Suárez de Peralta said that on the morning of the sixteenth of July a squadron of soldiers went to arrest Martín Cortés. They found him alone at his brother's house on the plaza and told him that the officials of the royal houses had sent for him. He reached for his cape and his sword, but the bailiff said he could not take his sword because he was going as a prisoner, not a guest. 'But why?' Martín asked. Was he feigning surprise, or did he know they had been coming for him? Suárez de Peralta does not say and probably did not know. He tells us only that the bailiff replied that his orders were to bring him to the royal houses and that was what he must do. At this Martín Cortés surrendered his sword.

The soldiers had brought a beautiful black horse for him to ride. It was his brother's horse, and he must have recognized it and guessed with growing apprehension how it came to be in their possession. They told him to mount it but once he was in the saddle they took the reins from him and tied his hands together. The bailiff placed two men on either side of him and positioned himself behind with several other soldiers. Then this solemn procession began its slow progress along the cobblestones of the street and out into the plaza.

According to Suárez de Peralta, people were shocked and dismayed at the arrest of this son of the city's first family. They stood in silence to watch Martín Cortés pass by, and as the soldiers led him across the plaza he felt the watchers' eyes on him. He was about to be imprisoned in the grandiose palace his own father had constructed in the aftermath of the Conquest, but he had little time to reflect on this forlorn irony. Suárez de Peralta, who learned much of what he knew from a priest attached to the royal houses, said that once inside those formidable stone walls Martín Cortés was told that his brothers, the Avila brothers and eighteen of their friends had been taken prisoner too.

The judges of the royal council had arrested the marqués earlier that day. They had no wish to provoke the uprising they feared was in place by arresting him in public, so they lured him into a trap. It had not been difficult to ensnare him. They had simply sent word that letters and documents had arrived from the king, and invited him to join them to hear what news they contained.

Juan Suárez de Peralta said the marqués had come riding eagerly across the plaza on the horse that would later be used to bring his brother to the royal houses. He entered the salon where the judges sat waiting and, as it was summer, and warm, he was dressed informally in a damask shirt and black jerkin, with his sword at his hip. 'What good tidings do we have?' he asked, as he sat down in the chair the judges had left vacant for him, but they ignored his question. Instead, one of them stood up and demanded his sword. It was only then that the marqués noticed the guards at the door. The judges told him he was a prisoner of the king. Suárez de Peralta's informant said he looked shocked and confused and seemed to think the order for his arrest must have arrived with the letters from Spain. He surrendered his sword. He was unarmed and alone and had no choice but to proceed under guard to the rooms the judges had prepared for him.

The Avila brothers had been resting in their mansion on the northern side of the plaza when the soldiers came for them. Suárez de Peralta said they seemed unaware of the danger they were in. Alonso de Avila had been wearing his usual fine and expensive garments, but Gil Gonzalez de Alvarado had just returned from one of his estates outside the city and was still wearing his rough clothes and spurs. They too were arrested and, as people gathered to watch, alarmed by what was taking place in their city, these young conquistador sons were taken in chains across the plaza to the royal houses. There they were charged with plotting to anoint the marqués as the king of New Spain.

My room in Mexico City is in a quiet street not far from the statue of the last Aztec emperor. From there it is an easy walk along the elegant Paseo de la Reforma to the gardens of Chapultepec, and through them to the steep and winding path that leads up to Chapultepec Castle. Inside the castle is a library named in honor of the great Mexican scholar, Manuel Orozco y Berra.

In 1830 he devoted many hours to the task of making transcripts of the original trial documents of Martín Cortés, and on a grey morning in October, high above the city in the castle library, I began reading through those transcripts. From them I learned what happened to Martín Cortés after he disappeared into the royal houses in July 1566. The marqués had been confined to an upper floor of the royal houses, as befitted a man of his station, but Malinche's son was taken to the public cells and imprisoned there with his brother, Luis, with Alonso de Avila, Gil Gonzalez de Alvarado, and the dean of the Cathedral. How did the five men in the cells spend the first of their many days and nights together? In anguish and fear, I suspected, as one by one they were taken for questioning by the judges.

Martín Cortés was brought before the judges on the day of his arrest. A scribe called Gordian Casasano was present to record his replies to the judges' probing questions. 'Don Martín Cortés, Knight of the Order of Santiago,' Casasano wrote, 'places his right hand on his breast and swears by God and Santa Maria and by the Habit of Santiago that he will speak the truth of what he knows.' After that the interrogation began.

'What is your name, how old are you, and whose son are you?' the examining judge asked.

'My name is don Martín Cortés,' he replied, and it startled me to hear this direct and simple statement from the reticent lips of Malinche's son. 'I am forty years old, more or less,' he continued. 'I am the son of don Fernando Cortés, and the brother of don Martín Cortés, the present marqués.'

He seemed unsure of his age, but his uncertainty cannot have been unusual for men and women of those times, especially those born, like him, in the aftermath of war. I noticed that he made no mention of his mother.

The judge asked him whether he knew don Luis Cortés and don Alonso de Avila.

'Don Luis is my brother,' Martín replied, 'and I have known him for many years, but Alonso de Avila for only three.'

The judge asked him whether he had heard talk of a rebellion or uprising in the city, and of plans to kill the members of the royal council.

'I have not heard any such talk,' he said, 'but some persons, whose names I cannot now recall, did say that they had heard comments along these lines which I took to be merely frivolous chatter and not worthy of consideration.'

The judge asked him what weapons he had gathered in the past few days and for what purpose.

'I have not gathered any weapons,' he said, 'only some harnesses for a tournament I wished to take part in, and I had intended to share them with other participants.'

'Who were those other participants?' the judge asked him.

'Don Luis de Ortega requested a helmet,' he said, 'and don Alonso de Estrada and some other soldier friends of mine asked for arquebuses. But I didn't obtain them until today.'

The judge asked him whether his brother, the Marqués del Valle, had suggested to him that on the day of the tournament they should kill the Audiencia judges and begin the uprising.

'No,' he replied. 'My brother never suggested any such thing. The purpose of the tournament was to celebrate the birth of his twins, and that is all.'

'Have you ever seen any persons talking in secret with your brother, the marqués?' the judge asked him.

'I have never seen the marqués speaking secretively with anyone,' Malinche's son replied, 'neither by day or by night, *de noche ni de dia*, although occasionally he withdraws to speak in private with a guest.'

Finally the judge asked him whether the marqués had ever said anything to him about that matter that he, don Martín, had described as frivolous talk.

'My brother thought the rumors and complaints about the king's proclamation were frivolous and without substance,' he said, 'but he feared they might cause harm. Therefore he scolded those he heard talking that way. He told them they had no cause for complaint because he was sure the king would soon remedy the situation.'

The scribe recorded all these answers, all these careful words. Yet what he could not capture with his quill and his ink and his neat lines of script were the pauses, the silences,

as Martín Cortés considered his responses, the sound of his
breathing, the sound of his voice, the expression in his eyes as
he spoke. Was he angry or calm or fearful as he stood before
the judges with his right hand on his breast? They had used
no violence against him during that first interrogation, but he
would have known that they could use it at any time they
chose. He signed his statement declaring it to be the truth by
the oath he had sworn, but was it? Had his brothers been
plotting against the Crown? Was he trying to conceal what
he knew?

Three days later he was still in the cells. On the third day
he sent a petition to the judges who had questioned him.
'Most powerful lords,' he began, 'don Martín Cortés, son of
the first Marqués del Valle, prisoner in these royal houses by
order of your lords, states that he has been imprisoned now
for three days without knowing why. He asks that your lords
either make clear the reason for his imprisonment, or set him
free.' The judges did neither. Six days later Martín Cortés sent
another request asking for release or clarification of his
charges, but once again they ignored him.

On the thirtieth of July they announced their formal
charges against him. They accused him of having known for
ten or eleven months that his brothers, the Marqués del Valle

and don Luis Cortés, along with don Alonso de Avila '*y otras muchas personas*' had been planning a rebellion and uprising against His Majesty. Martín Cortés had known this, they charged, yet despite the many privileges given to him by His Majesty and by his father he had concealed the plot from the authorities. In this Martín Cortés had committed a grave and atrocious crime against the Crown. It was a crime, the judges said, for which he deserved a great and severe punishment.

In the days and nights that followed, Malinche's son watched what happened to the Avila brothers, and learned how severe his own punishment might be.

The judges appointed lawyers to defend Alonso de Avila and Gil Gonzalez de Alvarado, but gave them only seven days to prepare the case. The lawyers asked for more time. The judges refused. They had sequestered numerous documents from the Avila house across the plaza. They had gathered testimonies from the informers and from several of the other alleged conspirators they had arrested. By the end of July they had sufficient evidence for their purposes.

Juan Suárez de Peralta heard later from the priest in the royal houses that on the evening of the third of August the judges had appeared in the cells below the royal houses to pronounce sentence on the Avila brothers. Suárez de Peralta said the brothers listened in shock as the judges told them they would be beheaded that night in the plaza, and that following their decapitation their heads would be mounted on pikes and left to rot as a warning to anyone who even thought about rebellion. Furthermore, their mansion would be demolished, the ground around it covered in salt, and in the midst of this salted wasteland a large painted sign would announce that this had been His Majesty's justice, carried out in his name by the royal council, against men who had been traitors to the Crown.

The priest who had been present throughout the sentencing told Suárez de Peralta that the twenty-five year old Alonso de Avila had put his trembling hand to his brow, turned to him, and asked, 'Is this possible?'

'Yes, señor,' the priest had responded. 'You should make your peace with God and beg him to forgive you your sins.'

'Is there no other way?' Avila had whispered. '*No hay otro remedio?*'

'No señor,' the priest replied, and on hearing this Avila had begun to weep.

The burning place for heretics, the *quemadura*, lay a few blocks west of the plaza, in the square of San Hipólito, close to the present-day Alameda gardens. But treason against the Crown required a more grandiose stage for its rituals of punishment. The plaza, in front of the royal houses and the metropolitan cathedral, and in sight of the Avila brothers' mansion, was an eminently fitting place for their execution. Their father had built the house in triumph in the aftermath of the Conquest. It would be the last thing they saw before they died, knowing they had lost what he had fought so hard to win.

Juan Suárez de Peralta described their deaths in terrible detail. He said that torches had been lit all around the plaza and a high scaffold constructed in its centre. Thousands of frightened men and women came pouring into the square, weeping and wiping the tears from their eyes with their handkerchiefs. Armed soldiers on horseback and on foot formed a wide path leading from the scaffold to the royal houses. At the appointed time the captain-general of the city rode down that path toward the royal houses. 'And I went with him,' Suárez de Peralta said, '*yo iba con él*, and we entered the door of the jail where the prisoners were waiting with their ankles in chains.' So he was not just a spectator. He was a member of their official escort and he never forgot what he saw that night.

Twenty years later, when he wrote his account of all this, Suárez de Peralta still recalled the clothes Alonso de Avila had been wearing on the night he died: velvet stockings, a satin doublet, a damask robe trimmed with jaguar skins, a cap decorated with feathers and pieces of gold, a golden chain at his collar, a tawny cape across his shoulders. In his hand he carried a rosary his sister, who was a nun, had given him. His brother, Gil Gonzalez de Alvarado, was still dressed in the rough garments and leather riding boots in which they had arrested him eighteen days earlier.

The brothers rode toward the scaffold on mules, and several Dominicans, who had come to help them die good deaths, walked beside them. The executioner followed behind the condemned men and the town crier walked ahead, playing a mournful tune on his trumpet. The procession reached the scaffold and, as the Avila brothers climbed up on to it, a moan, so great and eerie that it unnerved Suárez de Peralta, passed through the crowd.

He saw everything that followed from close at hand — 'lo vi y lo oí todo' — because throughout the executions his horse's nose was touching the edge of the scaffold. He said that Gil Gonzalez de Alvarado was the first to die. He seems to have accepted his fate, if not his guilt, for when he made his confession he assured the crowd he knew nothing of any rebellion. He received absolution from the priest beside him, and laid his neck on the block. The executioner, who Suárez de Peralta said was not a good exponent of his art, cut off Gil Gonzalez de Alvarado's head amid the sobs and cries of the watching crowd.

When Alonso de Avila saw his brother's head fall to the scaffold he looked shocked, as if he had not believed until this moment that he would really have to die. He fell to his knees in fright, Suárez de Peralta recalled and, whispering the penitent's prayer, '*Miserere mei, Deus*, have mercy on me Lord, in thy kindness …' he began fumbling with the cords of his collar. It was his duty to lay his neck bare for the executioner, but suddenly he stopped and gazed toward his mansion across the plaza and cried out, 'Oh, my children, my dearest wife, to think that I should leave you in this way!'

Suárez de Peralta said there were murmurs in the crowd, for in this ritual of death a man like Avila was expected to die courageously, not whimpering in fear. The priest reminded Avila that this was not the time for such a lament, that he should look to his soul in the hope that it would fly directly to the Lord. 'And I promise you,' the priest told him, 'that tomorrow I will say a mass for you.' He asked the men and women watching to commend Avila's soul to God and to urge him to declare that his execution was just and proper, as was correct at such moments.

The watchers below the scaffold understood their part in this ceremony and did as they were asked. They began praying aloud for Avila and called on him to make his confession. The priest turned and spoke gently to him, saying, 'That is the way, is it not señor?' He was prompting him, of course, in the etiquette of public death, for in spite of Avila's fine manners he had probably never thought to prepare himself for such an end. After several minutes of anguished silence Avila agreed that it was the way and, falling to his knees again, he began to pray.

Juan Suárez de Peralta said it was obvious to all who watched that Avila feared death terribly. He stammered out his confession, admitting his guilt but refusing to incriminate others, and when he had finished, he lowered the collar of his shirt. The executioner stepped behind him and tied a blindfold around his eyes, and Avila, confused, reached out and touched it with that trembling white hand of his. He whispered something to the priest at his side, something Suárez de Peralta could not hear. Then, at last, he laid his head on the block and prepared to die.

The executioner had to hack three times at his neck before he managed to sever it, and at each blow the crowd cried out in disapproval. Suárez de Peralta said that as they left the plaza everyone felt distressed and confused about what had happened, and nobody could make out whether the Avila brothers were, or were not, guilty.

Water and Rope

In the plaza later that week I saw a banner fluttering close to the place where the Avilas had died. A student handed me a pamphlet denouncing the bombing of Afghanistan. I found it difficult to concentrate on what she was saying, but we talked for a while and then I walked over to my friend at the Great Temple of the Aztecs and asked him if he could me show me where the Avilas' house had once stood. 'There,' he said, and he pointed down the wooden walkway that runs along the western side of the temple complex.

I followed his gaze and saw a small plaque high on the wall above the path. I bought a ticket to the complex and went in to read it. 'Here on the site of the Great Temple stood the house of the Avila brothers who, along with Martín Cortés, son of the conquistador, Hernán Cortés, were imprisoned on July 16, 1566 for conspiring against the Spanish Crown. The Avila brothers were condemned to death and beheaded on 3 August that same year,' it continued. 'The sentence ordered that their house be torn down and the ground covered with salt. After that the site remained abandoned for many years during which time it was used as a rubbish tip. These events were recorded on a plaque carved in the sixteenth century.'

The sign erected by the Spanish Crown in 1566 had disappeared centuries ago; now this bleak, modern plaque commemorated their downfall. Yet it mentioned only one Martín Cortés. I asked my friend at the Great Temple which brother he thought it referred to.

He looked toward the plaque, shaded his eyes, then turned back to me.

'I always assumed it meant Malinche's son,' he said, 'but now I'm not sure. Perhaps it was his brother.'

All afternoon Alonso de Avila's terror that night in August 1566 played on my mind. I thought about the crowd's dismay at his fear, and their confusion over whether he was guilty or not, and found it difficult to reconcile that long-ago calamity with the dancers in the plaza, with the balloon-sellers, with the young boy playing joyous salsa at his record stall.

Suárez de Peralta's shock at the sudden downfall of the Avila brothers still resonates through his words, even after so many centuries have passed. He said that in the weeks that followed the executions he often passed through the plaza and stared tearfully at the Avilas' rotting heads. They had been stuck on pikes above the gallows and a large nail had been driven through their foreheads and into their skulls.

They had lost everything, Suárez de Peralta said, 'life, honor and property, *vida, honra y hacienda*'. At twenty-five he was the same age Alonso de Avila had been when he died. Suárez de Peralta recalled how a few weeks before Avila's death he had seen him passing by on a fine white horse with his pages and his lackeys by his side. They had spoken together, he said, about some *pelota* games Avila intended holding in his house. To Suárez de Peralta that conversation seemed now like some lost and remote dream.

After the execution of the Avila brothers the judges turned their attention to their other prisoners. In September they questioned the marqués. The answers he gave were many and intricate. He denied that he had come to the 'Indies' for the purpose of rebelling and claiming them as his own kingdom. He denied that he had been conspiring to forge alliances with the French and with the Vatican and to make himself king of New Spain. He argued that it was not inappropriate for him to have a lance-page walk before him. He said the size of the controversial silver seal that had so angered the viceroy was not his fault; it was the silver smith's, because he had made the seal to the wrong dimensions.

The marqués said that he had gained few friends in New Spain since he arrived from the realms of Castille; on the contrary, he had acquired many rivals and enemies. He devoted more than half his eighty-eight responses to describing the enmity that existed between himself and his accusers. He recalled how in May the previous year of 1565 two of them had deliberately upset and harassed him in the street by not removing their hats or showing him respect. He described similar insults they had offered him on other occasions, and the frequent fights that had broken out between them in recent months.

My heart sank as I read his words, for they seemed to confirm everything Juan Suárez de Peralta had said about him. By his own account the marqués was a young man obsessed with his rank and his place in the city of Mexico. It did not prove he had been plotting to make himself king of New Spain, but it revealed how vulnerable his arrogance and his imperious airs had made him to such charges.

I wondered, as I had often wondered, how the marqués felt toward his half-brothers. And now this crisis had engulfed them, how did they feel toward him? I knew from the testimony of one of the accusers that the now-imprisoned Luis Cortés had referred to him as 'that little shit, *la cagadita*, the marqués', but the marqués said nothing about Luis in his responses to the judges.

He did refer to Malinche's son, however. He said it was true that don Martín had planned the tournament the judges alleged was a cover for an uprising. So he blamed his brother for this suspicious event. But he assured the judges that it had been intended to celebrate the marquesa's safe delivery of her twins, and nothing more. He said he had suggested that don Martín travel to the realms of Castille to represent the city's discontented conquistador sons in the matter of the king's new proclamation, and to negotiate for them at the royal court. In other words the marqués was at pains to show that he and his brother understood the correct channels for airing grievances against the Crown, and were not inclined toward inciting rebellion.

Finally the marqués said that during Holy Week he had feared that two of his accusers were planning something against him and had confided his concern to don Martín.

A few days later, on Holy Saturday, he felt certain his enemies were on their way to attack him in his house. He had asked don Martín, who was there at the time, not to leave him, because he was afraid they were coming to do him harm. 'And so don Martín was on his guard,' he said, '*y asi estuvo rrecatado el dicho don Martín.*'

Only four references, yet they suggested that despite that long and bitter property dispute I had seen in the Archivo General, the marqués looked to his older half-brother for advice and support, and knew he could turn to him for protection if he were in danger.

What did Malinche's son think of his brother, the marqués? Did he regret the haughty conduct, the airs and the graces that had antagonized the viceroy and the leading citizens of Mexico City?

He left no abusive comments, no lamentations or criticism about the marqués. He must have sensed the danger into which his younger brother was leading them, yet seems to have remained loyal to him, as his father would have wanted. Perhaps he loved his brother, in spite of everything.

Juan Suárez de Peralta said it was the judges' habit to deliver their verdicts to their prisoners after midnight and without warning. Knowing this, the men in the cells existed in a constant state of restless fear, unable to sleep in case the judges' secretary, accompanied by the chaplain, should come knocking at their cell door. Late one night toward the end of September these two harbingers of doom appeared at the cell of Luis Cortés, to tell him he would be decapitated in the plaza, not that night, but soon.

We do not know whether Luis cursed, wept and pleaded as Alonso de Avila had done, or whether his brother, Martín wept with him, for if Juan Suárez de Peralta heard anything about their responses to this sentence he kept it to himself. But Luis was the first of the Cortés brothers to be condemned and the news shocked the city. It showed that the judges were not afraid to touch the sons of Hernán Cortés.

In September Martín Cortés's own battle for survival intensified. That month his accusers reiterated under oath their original accusations. They swore that he had conspired with the marqués to kill the judges of the royal council and any guards who tried to prevent them. They claimed that he had met with the other conspirators in his brother's house, and that together they had plotted to

make the marqués king of New Spain. They said don
Martín had approved the plot, had given advice and assistance to the other conspirators. He had gathered harnesses
and armor on the pretext of organizing a tournament,
they alleged, and had told his soldier friends to say, if they
were asked, that their horses and their armor were purely for
that event.

Who should the judges believe? Who should we believe
almost five hundred years later? The trial of Martín Cortés
had become a question of who was more trustworthy —
he or his accusers. In October his lawyer called twenty-
seven witnesses to attest to his good character and his loyal
service to the Spanish Crown. Some of what they said
confirmed what I already knew. Other fragments of their
testimony threw a sudden glimmer of light on his new life
in Mexico.

They testified that when he was young his father, don
Hernándo, had taken him to Castille and placed him in the
service of the empress. After her death he had served the
prince, Felipe, 'until he could take the sword, *hasta que pudo
ceñir espada*', after which he had accompanied the emperor
on his journeys to Algeria and Germany. There he had been
wounded many times in battles and encounters.

The witnesses for Martín Cortés swore that he had always lived in devotion as a good Christian. They said that during the previous Christmas of 1565 he had been gravely ill, had confessed and taken communion many times. They said that for eight months prior to his arrest he had been occupied with negotiations for his son's marriage to the widow of a kinsman, Pedro de Paz. How old did this make his son? The usual age for a young man to be betrothed was around sixteen. As I thought, Fernando must have been born early in the 1550s.

Martín Cortés's witnesses said it was well known that when Alonso de Avila realized he was going to be executed he became greatly disturbed, lost his reason and talked nonsense but, when he did confess on the scaffold, he did not name don Martín as his accomplice, nor any other person. They said the accusers in this case lived bad lives and were notoriously bad Christians with many defects. The witnesses added that the accusers were known enemies of don Martín and of his brother. Their testimonies, therefore, could not be trusted.

Every morning that week I walked to the castle above the woods of Chapultepec, and every afternoon I returned depleted from my day's reading. My head and eyes ached and I felt trapped within the claustrophobic labyrinth of those old transcripts.

Years earlier I had studied the witch persecutions of sixteenth-century Europe and their final tragic outburst in Salem. I thought I saw a similar pattern of human behavior in the conspiracy documents, and felt as perplexed as the citizens of Mexico City must have felt in 1566. Was there or was there not a conspiracy afoot? If a plot did exist, was it against the Crown, or against the Cortés and the Avila brothers? When would the accusations and the counter-accusations, and the arrests they inspired, come to an end?

There was no reason to expect a miracle. Now that Luis Cortés had been sentenced to death it was clear the judge would spare no-one. Yet within days an unexpected reprieve came for Luis, and for the frightened people of Mexico City. A new viceroy, the Marqués de Falces, had landed at the port of Veracruz. He knew nothing about the conspiracy trials until he arrived off the coast of Mexico, for they had erupted after he left Spain. When he learned about the terror that had engulfed the capital, he sent an urgent message from the coast, ordering the judges to suspend all punishments until he arrived. Two weeks later, in mid October, he entered the city and took personal charge of the inquest.

The new viceroy was the third in a line of humane and intelligent aristocrats sent to govern the complex, troubled, newly multiracial society called New Spain, and like his predecessors he had been sent to bring an orderly peace to the region. He met with the informers, decided that their allegations of conspiracy had been exaggerated and encouraged them to retract their denunciations. He reviewed the death sentence against Luis Cortés and commuted it to ten years in the galleys off Oran, on the coast near Algiers. It was still a harsh sentence but it spared his life. Then the viceroy turned his attention to the disgraced Marqués del Valle. He listened to his story and, with the power and influence only a viceroy could summon, he decided to allow him to return to Spain and put his case before the king in person. The marqués would return in relative poverty, however, for the judges had sequestered the lands within his marquesado from which he had derived his fabulous income.

Five months later the marqués knelt before the viceroy and swore an oath of allegiance, promising to go before the royal court when he arrived back in Spain. In April he sailed for Castille with his wife, the marquesa, and his brother, Luis.

Juan Suárez de Peralta said they sailed in great sorrow, knowing they had lost everything their father had won for them forty years earlier. But Malinche's son remained behind, imprisoned in the royal houses.

※

Why did he not leave Mexico City with his brothers? The documentation offers no answer to this question. It is possible the release the viceroy had negotiated with the judges did not extend to Martín Cortés, and he was never offered the chance to flee. Or perhaps he chose to stay and face trial because he believed the worst was over, and that he would be exonerated. It is impossible to know what he was thinking in April 1567 as he watched his brothers depart for Spain, but if he had known what was coming he would surely have gone with them, if he could. He didn't go, however, and I walked the steep path toward the castle that final week in October, knowing what lay in store for him.

His ordeal did not begin immediately. Soon after his brothers sailed for Spain, he was permitted house arrest. He had been in the cells for almost a year. Where did he go when they released him? The Crown had confiscated his brother's palatial residence on the plaza, so perhaps he found refuge with his wife and daughter and son in the house of a friend, or went to his sister and her husband for shelter. His movements are unknown during this sudden interlude of freedom in May 1567 but, wherever he went, his relief at his liberation, at the cool spring air on his face, at the company of his family and whatever friends were permitted to visit him, must have been as profound as it was brief.

If he had stayed in Mexico City because he thought the new viceroy would protect him, as he had his brothers, he was mistaken. The viceroy was soon beset by his own problems and in no position to help Martín Cortés. The accusers in the conspiracy case had become panic-stricken at the dangerous light the viceroy's intervention had cast on their denunciations. In order to protect themselves they wrote urgently to Spain claiming he had prevented them from coming to the royal court to reveal what they knew of the plot.

The judges too were angry at the viceroy's interference in their judicial proceedings. They withheld his encouraging reports to Spain, but ensured that their own letters, complaining about the seriousness of the plot and the viceroy's dangerous leniency toward the accused, were delivered safely to the royal court. In the absence of his viceroy's reassurance, with the memory of the rebellion in Peru on his mind,

Felipe II took notice of their grievances. He dispatched a new tribunal of judges to New Spain to find out once and for all whether an uprising had been planned in Mexico City.

Twenty years later Juan Suárez de Peralta remembered their arrival in Mexico City in November 1567, and their names: Alonso Muñoz and Luis Carrillo. They ordered the immediate construction of special dungeons beneath the royal houses for the many prisoners they intended to take and, once the dungeons were ready, they launched a new series of arrests. The accusers who had unleashed the terror in the first place but later retracted their allegations, were the first to be taken.

Suárez de Peralta saw one of them in his cell after his interrogation. It was Baltásar de Aguilar, and Suárez de Peralta said he was a pitiful sight. They had left him smashed to pieces, '*le dejaron hecho pedazos*', and in his anguish Aguilar had changed his testimony once more. He told his new tormentors that the retraction he had sworn before the viceroy the previous year had been a lie. His original statement — that the Marqués del Valle and his brothers had been plotting against the Crown — was true after all.

The only Cortés brother left in Mexico City was Malinche's son. On the fifteenth of November the judges sent for him, but this time their arresting officers did not bring an elegant black stallion for him to ride into captivity. Instead they tied him to a donkey, with all the humiliating symbolism that implied, and led him like a common criminal across the plaza. Later that night Juan Suárez de Peralta went with all the other frightened citizens of Mexico City to the doors of the royal houses to read the names of all those who had been arrested. That was how he learned that don Martín Cortés, 'who was a knight of the Order of Santiago', had been taken into custody again.

Not even the energetic and inquisitive Suárez de Peralta could follow Martín Cortés into the presence of the judges in November 1567. But in the castle library at Chapultepec I saw that a scribe called Juan Martynez Çavaleta had signed every transcript from now on. So this otherwise anonymous man had been a constant witness to what happened to Martín Cortés after he was arrested for the second time.

The judges had prepared a confession for Martín to sign. It was an admission of all the original charges against him. Had he signed it he would have incriminated himself and his brothers. He refused to sign, so the judges consigned him to their new dungeons. He was now trapped beneath the royal houses with his accusers, in what must have been a bitter incarceration.

A week after his arrest the judges sent their secretary to tell him they were resolved to obtain the truth from him. Therefore they had sentenced him to 'rigorous torture by water and by rope, *rigoroso tormento de agua y cordeles*'. Baltásar de Aguilar, the former accuser who had been 'smashed to pieces' by his torturers, was still lying crippled in the cells. Martín Cortés would have seen him in his pitiful state and known what to expect.

The lawyer who had acted for his brother in their dispute ten years earlier, Alvaro Ruíz, now became Martín's advocate. He opposed the judges' sentence. They gave him until the second of December to prepare his case. When that day came Ruíz said his work was not complete, so they gave him until the ninth; on the ninth they extended his time until the fifteenth; on the fifteenth they gave him until the twenty-third. The adjournments went on and on as Ruíz tried desperately to save Martín Cortés from being questioned under torture.

Why were the judges so patient? Perhaps they were implacable rather than generous, for they knew they held complete power over their prisoner, and that every postponement could only prolong his mental agony. But they were acting within the law when they sentenced him to be tortured, so it is also possible they merely wished to proceed according to correct process.

On Christmas Eve Ruíz presented eighteen new character witnesses for Martín Cortés. One by one the eighteen swore under oath that after Malinche's son went with his father to the kingdoms of Castille in 1528, he was admitted to the Order of Santiago. He had always been a devout and faithful member of the Order, they said. They swore that he was not given to conversations and rejoicings, 'era persona apartado de conversaciones y regocijos', adding that although he lived in his brother's house he took no part in the infamous parties of the marqués. Most importantly, given the threat now hanging over him, they swore that for some years now he had been thin and weakened by his battle wounds, therefore torture would kill him.

The judges withdrew to consider this new evidence. The documents tell us that while they deliberated they ordered some bales of cotton belonging to Martín Cortés to be confiscated. His lawyer protested, saying they had left his client with nothing with which to live or even to continue his legal battle. The judges rejected his plea and went ahead with the sequestration of the cotton.

They remained silent throughout the Christmas week while Martín Cortés languished in the dungeons. On the first day of 1568 the lawyer, Alvaro Ruíz, requested permission for him to attend mass with other knights of the Order of Santiago. It is not clear whether the judges gave him leave to do this, but if they did his liberty was brief. He was certainly in prison on the seventh of January because, according to the documents in the castle library, late that night the judges sent their scribe, Çavaleta, to him once more.

Çavaleta had come to tell him that his interrogation under torture would begin that night without delay. He then returned to tell the judges he had delivered the news to their prisoner in person. 'Don Martín Cortés confirmed that he had heard it,' Çavaleta wrote, 'and will submit to the will of their lordships, *que se haga la voluntad de los dichos señores.*'

From the day I set out to follow Martín Cortés's path through life I had known what would happen to him. It did not make the reading of the transcripts any easier, and I felt ashamed of my apprehension, knowing all I had to do was read what he had been forced to endure.

Çavaleta said the judges took Martín Cortés to a place in the royal houses where the rack had been assembled. They showed him the apparatus they intended to use on him; they ordered him to reveal what he knew about the rebellion and give them the names of the conspirators. If he did not, they warned, he would be put to the torture. If he should sustain injuries or die during torture, it would be his fault and his responsibility, not theirs.

Çavaleta does not tell us how long Martín Cortés looked at the apparatus in front of him. He was, presumably, preparing himself as best he could, but preparing to endure the question of rope and water was not like going into battle. It would be an entirely private and internal war during which they would pin him like a moth to a board, and attempt to turn him into a thing rather than a man. He would hear no rousing words from his emperor. He would not feel the tense excitement of his fellow soldiers and be urged to bravery by their camaraderie. He would not hear the thousand voices encouraging him to bear his fate with dignity that Alonso de Avila had heard eighteen months earlier in the plaza. Torture was an act carried out far from the public eye and it required a more solitary fortitude.

Çavaleta said that when Martín Cortés responded it was to say that he had already spoken the truth and had no more to say. The torturers were Juan Navarro and Pedro Vaca: it seems strange that their names should have survived all this time. The judges ordered them to strip Martín Cortés's clothes from him, and they did as they were told. January in Mexico City is icy, and he must have shuddered from the cold, and perhaps also from fear and humiliation, as he stood naked in the chamber before the judges in their elaborate robes. The two men tied his hands together with a rope, and the judges asked him again to tell them what he knew. He replied that he had already told the truth and had no more to say, as God was his witness.

The men threw him onto the rack, jerked his arms back above his head and fixed the rope around his wrists to the end of the apparatus. They tied more ropes around the muscles in his thighs and to his ankles and his toes, and pulled those ropes through holes at the other end of the rack. Then they began twisting and tightening them, using garrottes to increase their leverage.

Çavaleta's careful and precise transcript cannot convey the sound as Martín Cortés's bones were dislocated, as the ropes burned and sliced into his limbs and toes, as his groans and cries escaped him. It tells us only that the judges again demanded he tell them the truth about what he knew.

'I have spoken the truth, *he dicho la verdad*,' he replied, or gasped, or whispered. 'I have nothing more to say, *no tengo más que decir*.'

The torturers turned the garrottes again and tightened further the ropes attached to his limbs. Martín Cortés may have cried out — Çavaleta does not tell us — but he remained resolute in his answers.

'I have spoken the truth,' he said. 'I have no more to say.'

The judges now ordered the 'question of water' to be added to his ordeal. One of the torturers forced his head back lower than his body, and held his nostrils to prevent him from breathing through them. The other pushed a horn into his mouth to hold it open. Then he began pouring a half-quart of water down his throat as slowly as he could.

Probably not even Martín Cortés could have described the drowning horror he endured as they poured and poured, or the shock of relief when they released his nostrils and extracted the horn from his throat. The judges asked him again to say and declare the truth of what he knew. How long did he cough and gasp before responding? Could he speak or did he whisper? The scribe notes only that after some time he managed to reply, telling them again that he had spoken the truth and had nothing more to say.

From this point on a terrible monotony invaded Çavaleta's transcript.

'And then, by order of the judges,' he wrote, 'a half-quart of water was poured into his throat and he was told to declare the truth about what he knew.'

After each pouring, each near-drowning, the men extracted the horn from Martín Cortés's throat and the judges ordered him to speak. His voice may have sounded different as he stammered and whispered and panted his replies, but Çavaleta said his meaning did not change.

'I have spoken the truth,' he gasped. 'I have no more to say.'

They forced his head back, and thrust the horn into his throat.

'And then by order of the judges a half-quart of water was poured into his throat ...' wrote Çavaleta.

'I have spoken the truth,' Martín Cortés responded.

They forced his head back and thrust the horn into his throat.

'And then by order of the judges a half-quart of water was poured into his throat ...' wrote Çavaleta.

'I have spoken the truth,' Martín Cortés gasped, but this time there was a desperate edge to his words, 'and by the Holy Name of God, *el Sacratisymo Nombre de Dios*, I will say no more even if you kill me.'

They forced his head back and thrust the horn into his throat.

'And then by order of the judges a half-quart of water was poured into his throat ...' wrote Çavaleta.

'I have spoken the truth,' Martín Cortés managed to reply, 'and I do not know anything more.'

They forced his head back and thrust the horn into his throat.

'And then by order of the judges a half-quart of water was poured into his throat ...' wrote Çavaleta.

'I have spoken the truth,' Martín Cortés whispered, 'and I have nothing more to say.'

Suddenly it stopped. Çavaleta recorded that after the sixth jug of water had been poured into Martín Cortés's throat he was so ill, so weak and exhausted, that the judges decided to suspend the torture for the moment and resume when their prisoner had recovered sufficiently to endure more. I took this to mean he could no longer speak, was perhaps barely conscious.

I could have read Çavaleta's transcript in less than thirty minutes if I had not felt so agitated. But how long did Martín Cortés endure his multiple chokings and dislocations, his rope burns and cuts, the bitter cold and his naked helplessness? His ordeal might have lasted two hours, even more, for the judges wanted to induce him to speak, rather than kill him. Çavaleta did not record the time at which the torture began, but when he signed his transcript at the end he noted it was then nine hours before midday, that is, three o'clock in the morning on the eighth of January 1568.

Thy Home is Not Here

In 1978 an American poetry professor called Elaine Scarry wrote a study of the effects of torture on the human soul. *The Body in Pain*, she called it, *The Making and Unmaking of the World*. She based her findings on the experiences of prisoners in Chile, Greece, Turkey and Indonesia. From them she had learned a terrible truth: that world, self and voice can be lost through the intense pain of torture.

Is that what happened to Martín Cortés as he endured the question of water and rope? Did he too lose his world, his self and his voice? Not quite his voice, for somehow he found the strength for those resolute replies under torture. Did he find it in the knowledge he was protecting his younger brothers? Or did his desire to survive sustain him and give him the power to remain silent?

He was the only one of the alleged conspirators to resist in this way. Baltásar de Aguilar, Cristóbal de Oñate, Bernardino Maldonado, Gómez de Vitoria, Chico de Molina — all were tortured, all incriminated themselves and others, and each man changed his testimony several times as he tried desperately to appease the judges. What made Martín Cortés different from so many of his fellow accused?

His war experience distinguished him from many of them. The Avila brothers had never had to fight for anything in their lives. Nor had Baltásar de Aguilar or Gómez de Vitoria or Chico de Molina, who was the dean of the cathedral. But Martín Cortés had been a soldier in the armies of the Holy Roman Emperor since the age of seventeen. He had been wounded many times in battle yet survived, and although his friends claimed he had been weakened by his injuries, it is possible this was a ploy to save him from the ordeal of torture.

He was probably lean, as they testified, but lean does not necessarily imply weakness; on the contrary it can suggest a taut and wiry strength. Certainly the marqués had felt confident in his brother's power to protect him from physical attack. Besides, the mental force and discipline of a seasoned warrior is not easily lost. Perhaps it was this above all else that sustained him in the torture chamber.

There is one other thing that differentiates him from his fellow accused. Martín Cortés was the only mestizo among the alleged conspirators. So was his fortitude a legacy of his famous mixed blood? From his father the grim tenacity of the Extremaduran, from his mother the contemplative force of the Native American? Is it possible to inherit such qualities from parents we have barely known? Is it possible, now, to speak of such racial essentialism?

In *The Body in Pain* Elaine Scarry defined the immorality of torture as an absolute. Her words are irrefutable in the context of our times. Yet, in spite of his sufferings, Martín Cortés might not have agreed. The judges who interrogated him that January of 1568 may have treated his body brutally, but what they did to him did not violate sixteenth-century notions of morality, either in the Old World or the New. His interrogators did not belong to death squads or secret police as torturers so often do today. They were learned jurists and for them, as for all Europeans at that time, judicial torture was a legitimate process of the old Roman law of evidence to which they still adhered.

It had no exemplary role to play in society, however, as

did public execution, which was a spectacle designed to educate and caution as much as to punish. Torture was different; its purpose was to extract information and to keep it secret until it could be acted upon. That is why, as Juan Suárez de Peralta noted, the judges had posted armed guards in the streets around the royal house after they arrested Martín Cortés for the second time: in order to prevent people passing too close and hearing his cries. But word soon spread through the city that inside the royal houses the judges had stripped Martín Cortés and dislocated his limbs. Suárez de Peralta said it was the greatest sorrow in all the land, *'que era una lástima la mayor de la tierra'*.

Martín Cortés lay in the dungeons all day and night on the eighth of January, and for many subsequent days and nights. His ordeal may have ceased for the moment, but not the pain from his torn limbs and damaged throat. He knew his torment could begin again at any time, and he lay in an atmosphere of terror, among men already facing execution. His accusers had reaped the whirlwind of their own shifting testimonies: five of them had now been condemned to death; two were sentenced to die that night.

The scribe, Juan Martynez Çavaleta, had begun the day in the torture chamber with Martín Cortés. Late that night he was still at work recording the last words of the two prisoners about to be executed. The first to die was Gómez de Vitoria. He had been a retainer to Alonso de Avila and, before he was taken from the cells to be hanged and quartered in the plaza, he told a long and intricate story, so intricate that at times it is difficult to follow. He recalled a dinner in the Avila household some time early in 1566. Both Avila brothers had been present, he said, so had Luis Cortés and several other men. During dinner they had discussed the king's ruling on inheritance, along with rumors that a rebellion like the one in Peru twenty years earlier might now be afoot in Mexico City. At some point someone had suggested that Alonso de Avila could go to Spain to plead with the king about the question of inheritance and, if that did not work, to the king of France for help.

Gómez de Vitoria said Alonso de Avila had showed little interest in the proposed mission, but a few weeks later his brother, Gil Gonzalez de Alvarado, had suggested to Gómez de Vitoria that the two of them should go to Spain together to see what was happening about the succession of 'yndios'. If the signs were unfavorable, Gil Gonzalez de Alvarado said, they could seek an audience with the king of

France instead, and persuade him to come to New Spain with his forces to help them. Vitoria said he had told Gil Gonzalez de Alvarado these were childish ideas, '*heran nynerias*'. Gil Gonzalez de Alvarado had called him a coward, so Gómez de Vitoria had relented and agreed to go with him after all. But Alonso de Avila had later cautioned him about becoming involved in his brother's plans.

Other names drift in and out of Gómez de Vitoria's last confession. His fellow-accused, Bernardino Maldonado, had been in Peru, he said, and had boasted he would carry out the uprising in New Spain by himself if necessary, without the assistance of the marqués or anyone else. 'But it was all a joke, *por cosa de burla*,' Gómez de Vitoria told the priest and the scribe listening to his last confession in the dungeons below the royal houses. 'It meant nothing,' he said, and there was a puzzled sadness in his words, as if he could not believe what had come of those idle boasts and grumbles that long ago night in the Avila household. Gómez de Vitoria told Çavaleta he could not sign his confession because his arms were injured. He meant that they had been dislocated because, like Martín Cortés, he had endured the torture of rope and water. But before going to his death in the plaza he swore and declared that what he said was true.

The man who died with him that night was Cristóbal de Oñate. He too had been a retainer to Alonso de Avila and, when first interrogated in May 1567, he had sworn he knew nothing of any rebellion. Later, under torture, he had incriminated many people, including Gómez de Vitoria. Now, in his final moments, Oñate retracted those forced denunciations and swore that what he had testified against his fellow-accused was untrue. His words must have seemed a bitter comfort to Gómez de Vitoria, if he heard them, for they came too late to save him. Oñate also swore that what he had said about the marqués, Luis Cortés and Alonso de Avila was false. 'The said Marqués del Valle, don Luis Cortés his brother, and don Alonso de Avila never said or spoke or wrote anything about going to France,' he said.

'And don Martyn Cortés, brother of the said marqués, never knew or heard anything,' he told the priest and the scribe 'and if anything has been said or declared against him, I swear that it is false testimony, and that this is the truth.'

Late the following night the scribe, Çavaleta, appeared with the priest and the executioner at the door of a cell shared by Baltásar de Aguilar and two of the other original accusers.

Juan Suárez de Peralta heard later from his priest friend that when Aguilar saw the executioner he fell to his knees, weeping and begging for mercy.

The men sharing Aguilar's cell were Pedro and Baltásar Quesada. They tried to console him by promising him masses and prayers for the salvation of his soul. They assured him that after his death they would take care of his family, but Aguilar was terrified and inconsolable. Suddenly, in the midst of his pitiful uproar, the scribe managed to convey to Aguilar that the executioner had not come for him at all, but for the Quesada brothers. Suárez de Peralta said the brothers stood in silence, shocked at their sentence, and Aguilar fell silent too. Pedro de Quesada turned to the priest and asked him whether he was sure about the sentence. 'Yes, señor,' the priest replied, and he urged Quesada to accept his fate gracefully.

The Quesada brothers, like the Avila brothers, had been greatly admired in the city, and Suárez de Peralta said the people waiting by the scaffold in the plaza were astonished when they saw them emerge from the cells. It was clear that someone was to be executed that night, but nobody had expected it to be them.

Suárez de Peralta said the brothers died like gentlemen and good Christians and, before they were beheaded, they told the crowd that their sentences were just. They had indeed been plotting a rebellion, they said, and had used the masquerade at the house of Alonso de Avila to convey secret messages and covert signs to their co-conspirators in the plot. But only those involved in the uprising had realized what those signs had meant. The others had not understood what was implied, and the men still imprisoned in the royal houses, including Martín Cortés, had been unjustly imprisoned. He knew nothing, they said, and was innocent.

Everyone in the plaza that night of the ninth of January heard the Quesada brothers exonerate their fellow prisoners before they died. Gómez de Vitoria and Oñate had made their confessions in the dungeons below the royal houses, but the lawyer, Alvaro Ruíz, knew what they had said. Perhaps he had loitered near the cells to listen, or perhaps he paid Çavaleta to show him their confessions. The precise movements of the lawyer and the scribe, these two urgent players behind the scenes, are hidden from us, but this was a world in which last confessions were taken seriously — by those who made them, and by those who listened — and Ruíz would have known they might save the life of Martín Cortés.

The following day Ruíz appeared once more before the judges. The secretary, Çavaleta, was there to record what he had to say. 'In the name of don Martín Cortés, professed knight of the glorious Order of Santiago, and prisoner in your royal houses,' Ruíz began with great solemnity, 'I request permission to present confessions made and declared by Cristóbal de Oñate, don Pedro de Quesada, don Baltásar de Quesada and Gómez de Vitoria before they were executed.' Ruíz handed the documents to the judges. 'I submit them to your lordships and request justice for my client.' The dead men's confessions were lengthy and convoluted. Çavaleta and Ruíz waited while the judges read and analyzed them, and downstairs in the dungeons Martín Cortés waited too.

Hours passed while the judges deliberated on this new evidence. It was late by the time they sent Çavaleta down to the cells to announce their verdict. Did Martín Cortés lie maimed on the floor as Çavaleta read his sentence to him, or did he drag himself to his feet to receive the news with dignity? We know only what he heard, not how he heard it.

'In the case of His Majesty's prosecutor against don Martyn Cortés, Knight of the Order of Santiago,' Çavaleta intoned, 'we condemn don Martyn Cortés to perpetual exile from all the Indies, *todas las Yndias*. We order that he depart from New Spain on the first ship leaving for the kingdoms of Castille, with an armed escort for which he will pay the full cost. We further condemn him to pay the sum of one thousand gold ducats, half to His Majesty's treasury, and half for the cost of his imprisonment here in the royal houses. Should he break any part of this judgment he will do so on pain of death.'

Martín Cortés had been fighting for his life for eighteen months. He had suffered imprisonment and the hunger, thirst and constant terror that went with it. He had been separated from his wife and children, and had watched his brothers leave for Spain. He had endured torture and seen his fellow prisoners go to their deaths in the plaza. He must have known that three of the four men executed in the previous forty-eight hours had exonerated him, so he had every reason to hope for a complete acquittal. Yet the judges had not acquitted him. Was he shocked or angry or grief-stricken, or all three? Çavaleta said only that from the darkness of his prison cell Martín Cortés acknowledged he had heard the sentence, '*el qual dixo que la oya*'.

He could have accepted his sentence of exile and prepared himself to leave Mexico with his life, at least, intact. Instead he decided to appeal. It was a dangerous path to follow. It might lead him to the scaffold in the plaza, and result in his head rotting on a pike in the sun and rain for weeks and months to come.

Does his decision to appeal tell us something about his feelings for the city his father had conquered forty years earlier — where he had found his sister, settled his wife and children and established a life he may have had no wish to leave? He must have been desperate to stay in Mexico, to take such a perilous gamble, for he knew the judges could well change their minds during the appeal process, and condemn him to death.

As if to remind him of what he might yet suffer, the killings in the plaza continued. The next man to die was Bernardino Maldonado, who had boasted he would carry out the rebellion by himself if necessary. His father of the same name had fought beside Martín Cortés's father during the Conquest. The younger Bernardino was beheaded in the plaza, and with his death another conquistador family came to a grievous and shameful end.

Toward the end of January seven more witnesses came forward to testify to the good character and lineage of

Martín Cortés. Two of them were old conquistadors called Francisco de Granada and Juan de Najera. With their fellow witnesses they swore that they knew don Martín. He was married to a lady of good standing called doña Bernaldina de Porras, they said, and with her he had a daughter called Ana. They did not mention his son, Fernando, who had been born to another woman in Spain.

The witnesses swore that don Martín and doña Bernaldina were very poor and in need because they had been sustained in this land only by what the Marqués del Valle had given them, and that line of support had now been severed. They also testified that don Martín was the son of don Hernando Cortés and doña Marina, who had played a principal role in winning Mexico and New Spain for Castille. It was the only reference to Malinche in any of her son's trial transcripts.

Five days later another alleged conspirator, Gonzalo Nuñez, was taken from the cells to be hanged and quartered in the plaza. Still Martín Cortés waited, increasingly isolated, in the dungeons. Even if he had wanted to withdraw his appeal and accept his initial sentence, it was now too late. At last, sixteen days after he was sentenced to perpetual exile, the judges sent Çavaleta down to the cells to announce their final judgment on him. What did he expect to hear as the scribe stood before him? News of an acquittal, a pardon, or the unthinkable — a death sentence? What he heard was that the judges had confirmed his perpetual exile from the Indies, and added the additional directive that he was now also banned from going within five leagues or twenty-five kilometres of the royal court in Spain.

So for the rest of his days he would be excluded from his birthplace in the New World, and also from the Old World environment in which he had been raised and educated. The judges must have believed his claims of impoverishment, however, because they had reduced his fine to five hundred ducats. They had found it in their hearts to grant him that one small act of mercy.

The squirrels that haunt the ancient trees in the woods below Chapultepec Castle looked hungry and forlorn, and rain dripped from the trees and branches as I walked back down the path that final afternoon in late October. I had spent the week within the castle walls. I had read dozens of testimonies. I had searched through accusations and counter-accusations, denunciations and retractions. Yet I still felt unsure about what, if anything, had been stirring in Mexico City between 1566 and 1568.

Had it all meant nothing, as Gómez de Vitoria said before he went to his death? If so, to what exactly had Alonso de Avila and the Quesada brothers confessed on the scaffold? If Gómez de Vitoria was sincere in his last confession, the fledging 'plot' had been nothing more than a cocktail of foolish boasts and rumors ignited by conquistador rivalries and the memory of the Peruvian rebellion. It seemed that Baltásar de Aguilar and the Quesada brothers had taken part in those early rumblings of discontent about perpetual inheritance, but then lost their nerve and fled to the royal houses with their denunciations in order to protect themselves. They had implicated dozens of their fellow citizens, including Martín Cortés, before becoming entrapped in their own accusations.

The marqués, with his pompous ways, his foolish arrogance and his family history of dissent, must have been an easy target for their denunciations. He may even have enjoyed flirting with the notion of being crowned King Martín I of New Spain. Yet I had no sense that he had ever committed himself to the fledgling conspiracy. Why would he? He had been blessed with royal privilege and had little to gain and much to lose by a rebellion. Luis Cortés, on the other hand, seemed often to have hovered at the edges of the dangerous conversations that had led to this misery. Was he an active conspirator, or merely an opportunist waiting to see what might happen?

What of Malinche's son? Those men about to die had sworn he was entirely innocent of the conspiracy. I did not think they had lied. Sixteenth-century Spaniards who had lost all else believed a true confession would win them a place in heaven. Yet Martín Cortés must have heard the dangerous talk swirling around his brother, the marqués. He must have known something, but he kept what he knew to himself and through his silence he protected everyone he knew.

In February Martín Cortés was granted house arrest in order to prepare for his voyage into exile. He was now forty-six, although he may have believed he was younger. I wondered how he spent his last days in the city of his birth. He was leaving the world, his mother's world, that his father had conquered. He knew he would never see it again. He might never see his family again either, for his financial plight — his massive fine and his obligation to pay for his own armed escort — would have placed a sea voyage well beyond their impoverished means. How would his wife and children survive in his absence? Probably only through the kindness of whatever relatives or friends they still had in Mexico City.

On the seventeenth of March Martín Cortés was still in Mexico, because that day he asked the judges through his lawyer for an extension of time before he must depart, on the grounds that he was still too ill to travel. Centuries later, when Manuel Orozco y Berra prepared the transcripts I had read in the castle library, he could find no judicial response among the documentation and, as far as I know, none has ever come to light. So it is possible the judges ignored his request and in ignoring it, confirmed that he must go.

That attempt to delay his banishment is the last we hear from Martín Cortés during his lifetime. The trial transcripts do not say when he left Mexico, but late in March 1568 a ship carrying other exiles is known to have departed Veracruz for Spain. It must have been a melancholy voyage, not just for the usual reasons of seasickness and anxiety over fresh food and water and devastating storms, but because of what had passed between its passengers in the preceding two years.

That tremulous accuser, Baltásar de Aguilar, was one of those on board. He had, in the end, been condemned to death, but had managed to have his sentence commuted to ten years in the galleys off Oran. The Marqués de Falces who, as viceroy, had tried to calm Mexico City, was a passenger, so were Luis Carrilo and Alonso Muñoz, the judges who had ordered Martín Cortés's torture. They too were now in trouble with the Crown, for when Felipe II learned about the chaos and fear they had caused in Mexico City he ordered them back to Spain to justify their handling of the affair.

Did Malinche's child sail in that forlorn ship of exiles? It seems likely that he did. If so, he was driven from his father's city precisely forty years after he left it to begin his childhood journey to the royal court of Spain. His last recorded statement was his bleak acknowledgment from the shadows of the dungeon on the tenth of January 1568 that he had heard the sentence of exile passed against him; that and the last words he had uttered under torture two days earlier. 'I have told the truth. I have nothing more to say.'

Exile

Granada

It was late October and, as the Day of the Dead drew near, the market-stalls of Mexico City were overflowing with votive candles, with tiny skeletons and orange *cempasuchiles*, the flowers of the dead. On my writing table I found a small chocolate skull a friend had left for me. She had inscribed my name on it in sugar as a gentle reminder of my mortality.

I thought of the souls who had passed through Martín Cortés's life in Mexico and Spain. The year he was tortured and sent into exile was also a terrible year for Felipe II. In July his only son, the prince don Carlos, died of self-inflicted injuries. In October Felipe's third wife, Isabel de Valois, died in childbirth, as his first wife had done. Isabel's baby daughter died with her, but Felipe lived on until the end of the century in his Escorial palace outside Madrid.

Malinche's daughter, Maria Xaramillo, must have died the same year as her brother, for early in 1570 a priest at the Church of La Santísima in Mexico City referred to her as recently deceased. He mentioned that she had left funds for regular masses to be said at his church, but for whom? For her brother, Martín Cortés? Or for her mother? The priest did not say. But Maria had three sons who bore the Quesada name, were still alive and living in Mexico early in the seventeenth century, and whose *probanzas*, or proofs of service to the Crown, are held in the Archivo General de Indias in Seville.

In 1568, in Guatemala, Bernal Diaz del Castillo completed the first draft of his great memoir *The True History of the Conquest of New Spain*. He had already reached what was then the great age of seventy and would live for another fifteen years. He heard from afar what had happened to the sons of so many of his comrades from those old glory days, and probably sensed more than anyone that the conquistador era of Mexico was over, and the reign of royal bureaucrats had begun. That same year the Inquisition charged his own son, Diego Diaz del Castillo, whose mother was a Mayan woman, with telling Guatemalan villagers it was not a mortal sin to stay away from church on Sundays. But this conquistador son must have argued his case with skill and care, because eventually the charges were dropped and he resumed a normal life.

In 1565, the year before Martín Cortés was imprisoned, the Dominican, Bartolomé de Las Casas, died at his monastery in Madrid. He had reached the extraordinary age of ninety-two — almost double the normal life span for men in those times. This early abolitionist had never ceased to fight for the welfare of the people of the Americas. He endured profound remorse until the end of his days, however, for supporting the enslavement of Africans so many years earlier because, as he wrote in his monumental *Historia de las Indias*, 'they possess the same powers of reasoning as the Indians'.

Cortés's chaplain and biographer, Francisco López de Gómara, never again saw his biography of Cortés published in Spain after it was banned in 1554. But two years later he probably heard with secret pride that it had been published in Venice and Rome. Had he lived until the end of the sixteenth-century he might have been equally proud, and perhaps amazed, to learn that in Mexico City a young mestizo intellectual called Domingo de San Antón Muñón Chimalpahin Quauhtlehuanitzin had begun translating it into Náhuatl, the Aztec language, for the Náhuatl-reading public. Around the same time it was translated into Arabic for the Ottoman Sultan, Murad III, in a work entitled *Tarih-I Hindi-I garbi*. But López de Gomara died in 1564, and did not live to see his book take wings in those other tongues, and other worlds, despite its prohibition in his own country.

His Náhuatl translator, Chimalpahin, as he is always known, said in one of his own tracts devoted to society and politics in central Mexico, that Martín Cortés Nezahual-zolotl, the son of Moctezuma who had sailed to Spain with Malinche's son in 1528, died soon after he returned to Mexico in 1530. Some Mexica, or Aztecs, killed him because they were envious of him, Chimalpahin wrote, *ynin can quipamictito yn Mexica ohtlipa ynic*. He also noted that Don Martín had brought a Spanish wife back with him, *ynin Espanola yn inamic quihualhuicaya*, but he recorded nothing else about her, not even her name.

Juan Suárez de Peralta, the young man who recorded the downfall of the Cortés and Avila brothers, left Mexico for Spain in his thirties. He spent the remainder of his days in the beautiful town of Trujillo in Extremadura, and his account of the conspiracy of 1566–68 was published for the first time in 1589. But after that it seems to have gone missing for four centuries until, in 1878, a Spanish scholar rediscovered it among the manuscripts of the Biblioteca Nacional in Madrid.

When Suárez de Peralta wrote his memoir of life in Mexico City he remarked that the Avila family had seemed doomed to extinction. He said that years before the two eldest sons, Alonso and Gil, were executed in the plaza, a younger son had drowned in a water closet. He also told the tragic story of the Avila sister. Her name was Maria, he said, and when she was a girl of fourteen or fifteen, she had fallen in love with a young mestizo servant in the family household. The boy had returned her love and the young pair, knowing their marriage would never be permitted by Maria's brothers, plotted to elope together. But when Alonso de Avila learned of his sister's plans he dispatched her lover to Spain and told her he had died, in the hope that she would forget him. She could not forget him, so Alonso de Avila placed her in a convent and urged her to devote her life to prayer.

Maria de Avila did devote her life to prayer. It was she who sent her brother the rosary he carried to the scaffold on the night he was executed. Many years later the mestizo servant she had loved came back from Spain, wealthy and successful. When she learned of his return she was overcome to think that her beloved brother had lied to her, and forced her to live her life in unrequited longing for her lover. Her sorrow was such that she hanged herself from a tree in the convent garden.

Doña Juana de Zúñiga, the second wife of Hernán Cortés, lived on in the palace at Cuernavaca after her son, the second marqués, fled from Mexico. Her three daughters by Hernán Cortés married into Spain's most aristocratic families, but her step-daughter, Catalina Pizarro, who had been legitimized with Martín Cortés, was not so fortunate. Cortés had left Catalina a generous inheritance in his will, but doña Juana pursued her through the courts until she won most of it back for herself and her daughters.

Fernando Cortés, the son of the first-born Martín Cortés, said in his *probanza* of 1592 that he had served the Spanish Crown as a lieutenant in campaigns in Milan and Lisbon. In 1585, by which time he must have been in his thirties, he had traveled to the 'kingdom of Peru' where he joined the service of the Count of Villar. While there he married and became a Gentleman of the Company of Lancers of the Vice-regal Guard. Three years later he led a series of sea-battles against an English pirate fleet that had been devastating what is now the coast of Ecuador. In 1589, according to his own testimony, he returned to New

Spain. There he served as principal judge in the city of Veracruz that his grandfather, Hernán Cortés, had founded in 1519.

I knew from the earlier investigations I had made into the life of Fernando's grandmother, Malinche, that a few years after he made his *probanza* the Inquisition in Mexico had charged him with bigamy on the grounds that when he married in Peru he already had a wife in Seville. It is unclear whether this was the bride his father had in mind for him during those marriage negotiations of 1565, and I never learned the outcome of the bigamy charge against him — whether it led to the loss of his judicial office, or where or when he died.

What of the wife of Martín Cortés, doña Bernaldina de Porras, and her daughter, Ana? Somewhere in the archives in Mexico City or Seville there may be a record of what happened to them — a note requesting permission to return to Spain, or asking for special favors from the Crown. The exile of their husband and father would have left them impoverished, but for the moment their fate remains another unanswered riddle in this story.

The brothers called Martín Cortés probably never saw each other again after they were separated in 1567. On his return to Spain the marqués was incarcerated in a castle near Madrid and permitted no visitors, and by the time he was released from prison five years later, Malinche's son was dead.

The Crown confiscated the marqués's great estates in Mexico. It fined him a crippling fifty thousand ducats and condemned him to perpetual exile from the Americas. After his release from his castle prison the marqués seems to have spent the rest of his days on the fringes of the royal court, living the idle courtier's life his father would probably have disdained. He died in Madrid in August 1589 at the age of fifty-seven and his son, Fernando, who was then in his thirties, became the third Marqués del Valle.

Fernando had been born and raised in Spain and, although Felipe II had restored the marquesado to him, he never crossed the ocean to Mexico to visit it. When he died he left no children, so the title passed to his younger brother, Pedro, one of the twins whose birth had inspired that ill-fated masquerade in Mexico City in 1566. Pedro Cortés y Ramirez de Arellano was the fourth and last Marqués del Valle. He returned to Mexico in 1604 but died twenty years later without heirs. Hernán Cortés's legitimate male line died with him. It had lasted only three generations.

later without heirs. Hernán Cortés's legitimate male line died with him. It had lasted only three generations.

Prisoners tortured, or 'broken' on the rack — that frighteningly adroit word — could be crippled forever. Or in time they might mend, depending on their own resilience and the treatments available to them. Martín Cortés's kinsman, the Extremaduran nobleman called Alonso de Monroy, was said to have dislocated his hip while escaping from the prison into which Queen Isabella had thrown him. Yet despite his injuries he had crawled to safety and lived to fight again.

Martín Cortés's son, Fernando, said in his *probanza* of 1592 that after his father returned to Spain in 1568 he became a captain and commander of a regiment during the War of Granada. So it seems his injuries had healed sufficiently to allow him to spend long hours in the saddle in a helmet and metal breastplate, to wield a sword and dagger, and to endure constant jarring to his shoulders and his arms during hand-to-hand combat. It also seems his loyalty to the Crown was never doubted in Spain.

The War of Granada of 1568–70 is remembered now as the Morisco Rebellion. The great French historian of the sixteenth-century Mediterranean, Fernand Braudel, called it the last desperate attempt of Islamic Spain to rise from the ashes before it was extinguished forever. He said he did not know whether to describe its endurance to that point as a long survival or a slow shipwreck.

After the fall of Granada in 1492 the mutual tolerance between Christians, Jews and Muslims, that had long distinguished Spain from the rest of Europe, began to change. Islamic Spaniards, the 'Moriscos' or 'little Moors', were forced to choose between religious conversion or exile. Those who stayed agreed to observe the Christian rituals of baptism, marriage and burial in public. But in the privacy of their homes they clung to Islam, and evolved an Arabic term specific to Islamic Spain to describe the double life they now led in order to stay in the land their ancestors had settled eight centuries earlier: they called it *taqiyya*.

In January 1567 tolerance of that poignant *taqiyya* came to an end. That month, as Martín Cortés lay imprisoned in Mexico City, Felipe II sent criers into the streets of Granada to tell its Morisco residents, in Spanish and in Arabic, that they must now desist from speaking and writing in Arabic. They must abandon their visits to the public baths where Christians suspected them of indulging in Islamic ritual under the pretense of washing. Morisco women, who had been the heart of Islamic resistance through their language, their traditional dress and their adherence to dietary custom, were told they must now cease to veil their faces. The Moriscos must finally and absolutely renounce their Islamic faith forever.

The tolerance ended as it always does when a dominant culture decides that a minority group in its midst is dangerous. Spanish Christians had long suspected the Moriscos of maintaining seditious contact with the Islamic kingdoms of North Africa just across the Strait of Gibraltar. With the advent of the Reformation, Spanish Christians grew to fear their Morisco compatriots might be collaborators with the Lutheran cause as well.

Soon after those grim proclamations were read aloud in the streets of Granada, the city's Morisco leaders sent an urgent letter across the Strait of Gibraltar to the Ottoman garrison at Algiers. 'Our enemies surround us like consuming fire,' they wrote. 'Our sorrows are too great to endure.' They begged the Ottoman commander to come and save their community from the persecutions they knew were on the way. 'Written in nights of tears and anguish,' they concluded, 'but with hope in our hearts; such hope as can survive amid the bitterness of the soul.' But no help came. On Christmas Eve 1568 the long-suffering Moriscos of Granada and the surrounding Alpujarra mountains rose up against the Spanish Crown.

The poet, Federico García Lorca, wrote plaintively and often of horsemen riding toward their death across the plains of Andalucia, as if he could foresee his own brutal murder in an olive grove near Granada in 1936. His solitary riders know that death is watching them from the towers of Córdoba, or from the glittering balconies of Granada. They see their destinations in the distance, but know they will never reach them.

In the spring of 1569 Martín Cortés rode to his death across the plains of Andalucia. His son said he went to Granada with don Juan de Austria who took general command of the Christian forces in April that year. It was a fitting collaboration. Don Juan was the boy known as Gerónimo who had accompanied his father, Carlos V, to his monastic retreat in Extremadura following his abdication in 1555. So these two illegitimate sons of famous fathers, one a mestizo knight of Santiago, the other a much-admired prince and half-brother to Felipe II, rode together to the War of Granada.

It was a conflict noted for its atrocities as each side unleashed its long-simmering hatred for the other. Fernand Braudel said that on the coast below Almeria, Moriscos sold their Christian captives to Berber corsairs, while in the market-place at Granada Christians sold their Morisco prisoners into slavery. The Ottoman garrison at Algiers did send help, but not until 1569. By then the rebel cause was lost, and in the aftermath of that brief and savage war Felipe II and his advisers resolved to send the Morisco survivors into exile as far from Granada as possible. They decided they would march them to the north and scatter them among the Christian provinces of Galicia and Asturias where they could be watched for signs of treachery.

Exile, *exilio*. Whether in English or in Spanish it is a very small word for such a sorrowful and universal human exper-ience. In December 1570 the last Moriscos of Granada set out on their forced march toward the north through the icy mountain passes of the Sierra Nevada. Twenty-five thousand died along the way and their suffering seems to have affected the young don Juan de Austria, whose task it was to oversee their expulsion. 'I do not know if one can find a more moving picture of human misery,' he wrote to one of his brother's advisers, 'than seeing so many people setting out in such confusion, with women and children weeping, and so laden down with burdens.'

Martín Cortés probably did not live to see that terrible exodus of 1570. According to his son he died the previous year. Fernando Cortés did not say where, probably because he never knew, but he believed his father had been fighting with don Juan's forces when he was killed. Don Juan's field of operations during 1569 was the Almanzora Valley. So it seems that is where Malinche's son, 'the first mestizo', died and where his bones were scattered: in that beautiful eastern corner of Andalucia, in a valley high above the Mediterranean, closer to Africa than to Mexico.

Tepoztlán

The mythopoetic possibilities of Martín Cortés story
have not been lost on Mexico. The fact that the European conqueror of Mexico had two sons of the same name
— the first by his Amerindian concubine, the second by his
aristocratic Spanish wife — the fact that the mestizo son
suffered for his half-brother of 'pure' Spanish blood, and was
exiled forever from his mother's land — all this seems to
resound with forlorn metaphorical meaning for our post-
colonial times.

In 1974 Alejandro Galindo made a film he called *El
Juicio de Martín Cortés: The Trial of Martín Cortés*. In it the
brothers called Martín Cortés are assigned, like actors in a
miracle play, to the roles of good and evil for which they
seem to have been preordained from the moment they came

into the world. The eclipse between them is profound. Malinche's dark-eyed and valiant son is the good twin; a man so tormented by his mestizo identity, and the taunts of his brother, that in a moment of anguish during the film's closing scenes he kills his effete evil twin. The theatre audience within the film, which takes the form of a play within a play, looks on with sympathy and understanding. They know that what they have witnessed is an exemplary tale about the old colonial tensions between long-suffering copper-skinned Mexico and imperious pale-skinned Spain.

Two decades after Galindo made his film, Mexico's great twentieth-century writer, Carlos Fuentes, wrote a collection of stories called *The Orange Tree,* in which he too invited readers to contemplate the tragic tale of the sons of Hernán Cortés. Martín 1 and Martín 2 he called them with deliberate irony, since Martín 2 is the older brother and Martín 1 the younger. 'I am the first-born but not the heir,' Malinche's son tell us. 'I should be Martín the First, but I'm merely Martín the Second.' He speaks with the soft cadence of Mexican Spanish, rather than the strident tones of Castille, and he remembers his mother, Malinche. 'What more could I want than to be king of this land?' he asks her in a moment of prayer, as he dreams of a New World free of the Spanish imperial yoke. His loyalties lie firmly with her people — his 'brothers and sisters' he calls them — as he observes their suffering in the post-Conquest world of Mexico-Tenochtitlán.

In Fuentes's book, as in Galindo's film, Martín Cortés is a tragic victim of two cultures — a man torn between the Old World and the New, between his Spanish and his Amerindian lineages. In the age of identity politics, of 'blood and belonging' in which we live now, it seems a logical way to understand his story. But is it possible we assume a painful schism where none existed? What if the truth about Martín Cortés is more complex, and therefore more elusive? We may choose to define him by his mixed race, and to remember him as the first mestizo in a land of mestizos, yet as we gaze back at him across the centuries we cannot know for certain what his dual ancestry meant to him, or even whether it meant anything to him at all.

His presence among the accused, together with his famously heroic conduct, has tended to distort later interpretations of this episode in Mexican history. I have heard the conspiracy described as a mestizo rebellion against the Spanish Crown. The idea that it was based on racial lines and inspired by the noble ideal of independence has powerful resonance for modern Mexico, where Spain has long filled the role of official enemy in the national story. But it is clear from the identity of both the accusers and the accused that, with the exception of Martín Cortés, it was not a mestizo uprising. It was an affair between men of Spanish blood: a saga of warring conquistador families consumed by their own rivalries, and angered by what they saw as the tyranny of the Spanish Crown.

In that sense it was an unconscious prelude to, or rehearsal of, Mexico's later nineteenth-century independence war against Spain. That movement too would be led by men of Spanish blood, with mestizo and Indigenous Mexicans permitted only a symbolic role. But while the nineteenth-century independence movement aspired to the noble ideals of liberty and equality, the only freedom the discontented conquistador sons of Mexico City desired in 1568 was the freedom to enslave others, which was a freedom the Spanish Crown had taken from them. Yet the loyalty and personal courage of Malinche's son is no less astonishing even in what looks to us, five hundred years later, like an unjust cause.

In a quiet alcove beneath the atrium in the Archivo General de la Nación I found a public telephone. I glanced at my notes, rehearsed under my breath what I wanted to say, and dialed a Mexico City number. After several rings a man's voice answered. I introduced myself, taking great care with my Spanish, and he listened as I explained why I had called. 'Yes,' he said, he would be happy to see me to discuss his father's life and work. He suggested we meet the following day.

Next morning, in a train racing through the metro tunnels beneath the city, I marveled that a direct descendant of Martín Cortés, of La Malinche and Hernán Cortés, should be waiting for me at the other end. I had not been able to judge his age through his voice alone. I wondered if he had children, or whether he was the last of his ancestor's line. All I knew was that his father was Federico Gómez de Orozco, the historian who had described Martín Cortés's separation from his mother at the age of two.

I found the address he had given me, but the building had several levels. I stood outside, uncertain what to do next. Men and women came and went through the busy entrance and finally one of them came toward me. 'I think you rang me yesterday?' he inquired courteously. We took the elevator to his apartment on an upper floor. In the living room, a boy sat working at a computer. It was his son. He looked up as I entered and I saw that he was dark like his father, dark with deep brown eyes.

In the hours that followed we discussed the life and work of Federico Gómez de Orozco. Four days earlier, just a few blocks away in nearby Tizapán, an elderly man had told me he remembered don Federico.

'I can see him as if it were yesterday,' he had said.

'He had a moustache, he was a little rotund, and he would walk down the street here,' he had gestured toward the lane in front of us, 'puffing on a cigar, and always deep in thought.'

'We addressed him as "*maestro*", because he was such a learned man,' the old man added. 'Everyone respected him greatly.'

Federico Gómez de Orozco's son, Carlos, also recalled his father's rotund figure, the cigar, the moustache, the vivid intellect, while his son, Pablo, who was too young to have known his illustrious grandfather, sat listening. We talked about don Federico's gift for paleography and his contributions to the historiography of Mexico. We discussed his studies of Aztec papermaking, of Italian-born conquistadors, of Cortés's expedition to the Moluccas. Carlos described Sundays at his parents' house in Tizapán — long afternoons during which Mexico's finest scholars and artists, men like Iglesias and Granados, Rivera and Clemente Orozco, had gathered to discuss history, archeology, art, language, politics, their country's past and its future.

Carlos had been a small boy in 1944 when his father took part in the interment of Hernán Cortés's remains in the wall of the church of Jesus Nazareno. He did not recall his father talking about that ceremony. He did remember him building castles for him in the garden, and entertaining him with miniature soldiers and horses.

I told Carlos and Pablo what I had learned about their ancestor, Martín Cortés. I described the records of his admission to the Order of Santiago, and the lists noting his position as a page to the empress and the prince at the royal court of Spain. I told them about the long property dispute with his brother, about the trial transcripts, and the testimonies of his friends as they sought to save him from torture and execution and, in the end, from exile.

Martín Cortés's friends had described him as loyal, devout, courageous and silent, and the transcripts of his torture seemed to bear out what they said. Was his reticence the famous reticence of the 'Indian', or the reticence of the perfect European courtier as prescribed in the books of 'courtesy' he had studied as a pageboy? Whatever the source of his reserve, the comments of his friends suggest he was a serious and contemplative man.

Twenty years after the death of Martín Cortés a young chronicler in Mexico City named Dorantes de Carranza described him as a gentleman of courage and discretion, *un caballero muy discreto y valiente*. Four centuries later, when Manuel Orozco y Berra prepared his trial transcripts for the castle library, he called him *digno y cumplido* — dignified and correct, or dutiful. They were precisely the qualities expected of a member of the royal court of Spain.

I felt grateful for the records of those critical years of his life, yet I knew they could not capture the multiplicity of the man who was Malinche's son. I never saw him smile or dance or fall in love, laugh or yawn, or act ignobly. I had no impression of him as a husband and a father, except that like any European or Amerindian noble he had tried to negotiate a good marriage for his son. Did he carry a sense of loss about him? Did he walk through the great plaza of the city of Mexico with the air of someone who knew he was in danger?

The documents I had found offered glimpses of him as he passed, nothing more.

I had one question that I hoped his descendant, Carlos, could help me with, however. A genealogical chart Federico Gómez de Orozco had published at the back of his biography of Malinche, had shown a son born in 1930 whose name was Fernando. I wondered whether that son was still alive.

Carlos shook his head.

'He died of typhoid fever at the age of nine,' he said. 'He was my parents' only child at that time, and they were grief-stricken.'

'But I never knew him,' he added. 'I was born twelve months after he died.'

So Martín Cortés's line had faltered, had almost been extinguished, during that desolate year of 1939. But Carlos had four children. The family had survived into yet another century.

There was one last possible connection I wanted to explore. I took an early bus and passed once more through the veil of opaque air enveloping the capital. On the other side of that curtain the mountains and valleys of Morelos glistened before me in the morning sun. I saw pristine snow on the upper slopes of Popocatépetl and, as always, a thin trail of smoke drifting upward from its crater. Before long, the jumbled shapes of the Sierra de Tepoztlán came into view and below them the village of Tepoztlán.

In 1932 the American poet, Hart Crane, began his last, unfinished poem in Tepoztlán. 'Exile is thus a purgatory,' he wrote, 'not such as Dante built …' It was the final year of his life, and in his letters he described long days searching for fragments of Aztec idols in the cornfields around the village. He called the people 'pure, unadulterated Aztec', but in this he was mistaken. The people of Tepoztlán had been subject to the Aztec tributary empire when the Spaniards arrived; they spoke, and some still speak, the Náhuatl language, but they were Tlahuila, not Aztec.

I followed a steep path down through avocado and zapote trees toward the plaza of Tepoztlán. In the distance I could see the bell-tower of the church of La Santísima, and the white temple of Tepozteco on the basalt cliff above. By the time I reached the church the temple looked so close I felt I could reach up and touch it.

A man was watering plants in the churchyard. He

paused for a moment to follow my gaze toward the mountains in the distance.

'La Sierra de Tepoztlán,' he murmured.

Its jagged red and purple peaks stretched like a serpent across the horizon. I looked up at the church beside us with its bell-tower, its walls of the volcanic stone they call *tezontle*, its solitary stained-glass window.

'La Santísima looks very old, señor,' I offered.

He nodded.

'It is. But it was not the first church on this site,' he replied.

'There was an earlier one?' I asked.

'Yes,' he said. 'It was destroyed.'

'An earthquake?'

He looked out toward the sierra before replying. 'No,' he replied, 'the people tore it down some time in the sixteenth century. They were angry because the priests had destroyed the idol of Tepozteco.'

'That's his shrine up there,' he continued, pointing toward the cliffs above us. I looked and saw the temple gleaming white in the sun.

I asked him whether it was true Martín Cortés had been connected in some way to this church.

He nodded. 'They say he built it.'

He built it? Had he given funds for its construction, the way his father had paid for the construction of churches and monasteries and hospitals in Mexico City? The man didn't know.

We talked for a few minutes more before I entered the cool and shadowy chapel. Its ten cedar pews had been carved with motifs of the Holy Spirit, and its main altar was dedicated to the Holy Trinity, La Santísima Trinidad. I sat silently in the dark interior as an ancient villager lit candles before a small side altar to Our Lady of Guadalupe. When I left she was still praying in Náhuatl before the Madonna with the Indian face like hers.

At the café across the street I took a chair at a table covered with a turquoise cloth. The waitress was a young girl and I was her only customer. She said she didn't live in Tepoztlán. She came by bus each day from a smaller village in one of the valleys to the east, below the sierra. She told me she enjoyed her work.

'People come from *la capital*,' she explained. 'And sometimes from even further.'

I sipped the lemon tea she had made for me.

'Well, Tepoztlán is beautiful,' I said.

'It is,' she agreed, 'and very historic.'

She was quiet for a while, but when she spoke again she took my breath away.

'They say it once belonged to the son of Hernándo Cortés,' she said.

I looked up at her.

'His house stood right here,' she added. 'But this,' she pointed to the stone arch beside her, 'is all that remains.'

I saw that the archway was indeed old. It had been painted cream, and it led into a dark, interior courtyard.

'Do you know the son's name?' I asked her.

'Yes,' she nodded. 'It was don Martín Cortés.'

Some customers entered the café at that moment. I waited as she served them and when she returned to my table I asked whether she knew there had been two sons called Martín Cortés.

Her eyes widened.

'I had no idea,' she said. '*Que raro!*'

'It is strange,' I agreed, and I told her about Hernán Cortés with his parallel families of legitimate and illegitimate children.

'I wonder,' I asked her, 'do you know the name of don Martín's mother?'

She shook her head, 'But,' she added, 'some people say she was La Malinche.'

The window shutters were open wide. I looked out across the narrow street toward the church, the mountains and the valleys beyond. If what she said was correct, this is what he saw each day that he spent here. That blue haze of infinite distance and, if he turned toward the north, the watchful pyramid on the mountainside above the village.

'There are still people here called Cortés,' she told me as she took my empty cup. 'Perhaps you could ask them about don Martín?'

She told me how to find the one man she felt sure would be willing to talk to me. I found the steep cobbled lane she had described for me and walked uphill for fifteen minutes, past garden walls hung with crimson bougainvillea, climbing higher and higher until I drew level with the temple of Tepozteco in the distance. I stood looking out at it, and as I did a small boy caught up with me. I asked him if this was the way to the house of don Francisco. He said it was. We walked on together, talking, and a few minutes later the boy paused beside a wooden gate.

'That is don Francisco,' he pointed to a tall man tending an old zapote tree in his garden.

The boy called to him. Don Francisco stopped what he was doing, wiped his hands on a cloth and came toward the gate. He had never set eyes on me before, but he asked if I would like to sit in the shade of his verandah. He pulled out a cane chair for me and when he took off his hat I saw that his hair was white. His wife came out of the house to see who was there. We shook hands, she slipped back inside and returned minutes later with a jug of iced water and three glasses. Then she too sat down.

On the wall behind us I saw a painting of a man in the broad-brimmed sombrero, tapered trousers and gun belt of a Mexican revolutionary. He stood erect, looking sternly out from the picture.

'Agustín Cortés,' don Francisco said, nodding toward the picture. 'He fought beside General Emiliano Zapata during the Revolution.'

He went inside the house and returned with a small volume by Valentín López Gonzalez. Within minutes he had found the page he wanted. It was headed 'Assassination of Emiliano Zapata'. 'His faithful comrade Agustín Cortés remained at his side,' don Francisco read aloud, 'and at the moment Zapata fell, he too was assassinated.'

'Agustín Cortés was my uncle,' don Francisco said. 'He died with Zapata.'

I knew that this state of Morelos had been the heart and soul of the Mexican Revolution.

'Did you ever hear of my uncle?' don Francisco asked me, and I confessed that I hadn't, until now.

'The history books forget him,' he said closing his cherished volume and placing it on the seat beside him. 'But he was a great man.'

I watched a hummingbird flutter against the bougainvillea, draw in its quota of honey and move to another flower.

'How can I help you?' don Francisco asked me.

I told him I had come because I was investigating the life of Martín Cortés. I had heard that he, don Francisco, might be a descendant of don Martín and wondered if this was true.

He sipped some water and replaced his glass on the table. 'As far as I know his blood doesn't flow in my veins,' he said after some minutes. 'But there is a relationship between us.'

He paused for a moment.

'You know the church of La Santísima?' he asked.

I told him I had visited it that morning.

'I don't know if what I'm going to tell you now is true, but the story goes that not long after the Conquest the Indians began plotting a rebellion and one day they attacked the church. They tore it down, smashed it to pieces and everything inside it — the cross, the statues, the candlesticks. Then they fled to the hills behind the temple.'

He looked out into the garden, then back at me.

'Martín Cortés sent his men after them. They dragged them back here to Tepoztlán, and herded them into the plaza. It was night; the villagers had no way of escape. He announced that he would now put every one of them to the sword, every man and every woman who had taken part in the desecration. But he would spare their children. That was his one act of mercy. He would let their children live, but from now on they must bear his name.'

'I'm descended from one of those children,' he said. 'That, as I understand it, is how I came to bear his name.'

I had listened in silence.

'I'm sorry to tell you this,' he said gently. 'It's probably not what you wanted to hear.'

'It's not,' I replied. 'But I have to hear it.'

On the bus back to Mexico City that evening I thought about what don Francisco had told me. It was a terrible story. I had longed for multiplicity in my understanding of Martín Cortés. It seemed that in Tepoztlán I might have found it.

Could Malinche's son have behaved with such savagery toward his mother's people? I knew he could. He was a soldier and, like any sixteenth-century warrior from the Americas or Europe, he would have shown no mercy to anyone who crossed him. Sparing the children's lives might even have been seen as an act of rare clemency in his time. But why would he insist they take his name? Could it be because he shared his father's preoccupation with continuity, with 'memory'? If so, the massacre had worked: his chosen 'descendants' in Tepoztlán had not forgotten him.

Yet something troubled me. I felt a deep regard for the fine old man who had told me his unbearable tale, and I did not doubt his sincerity. I knew from experience, however, that elements of the oral tradition can be lost or reconfigured down the centuries until they tell a different narrative. I had little time left in Mexico, but I decided that before leaving I must try to verify don Francisco's story.

I made inquiries at the parochial office in Cuernavaca

but the records offered no precise dates for the church of La Santísima, and no way of comparing the timeframe of its construction with the four years Martín Cortés was at liberty in Mexico. I turned to a work by the ecclesiastical historian, Agustín Dávila Padilla, and learned with interest that, more than any other village or town within the Cortés marquesado, Tepoztlán had been known for its fierce resistance to Christianity.

Around the middle of the sixteenth century, I read, a Spanish priest — a Dominican like Las Casas — had destroyed the great idol of Tepozteco. He had hurled it from the cliff on which the god's temple still stood. In their anger and distress the villagers had attacked the church the priest had recently constructed; they had torn it down, stone by stone. Dávila Padilla did not name the church in question. Nor did he give the year in which those mutual desecrations of pagan idol and Christian chapel had occurred. Yet the fundamentals of this story suggested those events might well have been connected with the massacre.

I remembered a Cortés family document I had brought with me from Spain. It was a copy of the last will and testament of the second Marqués del Valle. I had ignored it until now because it was Malinche's son, rather than his half-brother, who had always been the object of my fascination. I retrieved it from my bookshelf, sat on my bed and began to read.

It was clear from his will that the marqués still possessed abundant riches when he died. He left his wife and children rich carpets, silver plates and goblets, diamonds, pearls and handsome garments. He left a crucifix and prayer book, and asked that every year on the sixteenth of July — the anniversary of the day he had been arrested in Mexico City — a solemn mass should be said for him. I noted that he freed several of his African slaves, and gave instructions for certain sums of money to be paid to five villages within the marquesado that had once been his. He listed Cuernavaca, Toluca, Teucalcingo and Coyoacan. He also nominated the village of 'Tepustlan'. It took me some minutes to realize he had meant 'Tepoztlán'.

'I declare that I owe the Indians of my village of Tepustlan six hundred and fifty gold pesos,' he said. 'I order that by way of payment they be released from the tribute they pay each year, and that the governor of the marquesado shall no longer collect such tribute from them. I further order that a sum of six hundred gold pesos be shared among the widows and the old and the poor of the village, for the work their people have carried out on my house in Cuernavaca.'

He had called Tepoztlán his village. I read the clause through once more to be certain. As I had suspected, Malinche's son had never owned Tepoztlán. Like every other town in the marquesado, the village had belonged to the half-brother who had shadowed him throughout his life.

***

I felt absurdly relieved to learn that it was the marqués who had owned Tepoztlán; that it was he, therefore, who was more likely to have been responsible for the massacre of villagers. Throughout my search for Malinche's son, I had prepared myself to deal dispassionately with whatever unpalatable detail might emerge about him. But the human desire for heroes and villains is very hard to resist, and I understood that night in Mexico City that I was as susceptible as anyone else to its influence. I realized that I wanted very much to absolve the 'first mestizo' of the atrocity at Tepoztlán.

I still don't know for certain what happened in that beautiful valley beyond the volcano, but I suspect a slaughter connected with the desecration of the church did occur during the early years of the Conquest. Whether Martín Cortés was involved and, if so, which Martín Cortés

— one or both — has so far continued to elude me. I go on searching for evidence that might solve this final riddle, and I sometimes fear what I may find. But I take courage from Voltaire's advice: that to the living we owe respect, to the dead we owe only the truth.

Bibliography

Manuscript Sources

Archivo General de Simancas, Valladolid

References to Martín Cortés, Malinche's son, as a page to the empress Isabel and the prince, Felipe, are in Legajo 31 No. 55 Casa Real Imperatriz and Legajo 35 No. 28.

Archivo Historico Nacional, Madrid

Documents concerning Martín Cortés and the Order of Santiago are in Caja 418 Expediente 2167.

Archivo General de Indias, Seville

The *probanza*, sworn in 1592 by Fernando Cortés, the son of Martín Cortés, is held in Patronato Legajo 17 Ramo 13.

Archivo General de la Nación, Mexico City

The lawsuit between Martín Cortés and his brother, the second Marqués del Valle, are held in Hospital de Jesús Legajo 300 Expediente 117.

Printed Sources

What follows is a list of the texts I found most helpful in preparing this book. Many are available in English. All are engaging works.

BERNAL DIAZ DEL CASTILLO's superb eye-witness (or 'I' witness) account of the Conquest of Mexico — *A True History of the Conquest of New Spain* — has never lost its ability to captivate readers. In preparing this work I have used the edition prepared by JOAQUIN RAMIREZ CABAÑAS (Mexico: Editorial Porrua, 1966) and entitled *Historia Verdadera de la Conquista de la Nueva España*. An abridged English translation has been prepared by J.R. COHEN under the title *The Conquest of New Spain* (Penguin, 1963).

FRANCISCO LÓPEZ DE GÓMARA's *Historia de la Conquista de México* was one of the non-participant narratives of the Conquest that enraged Bernal Diaz del Castillo and inspired him to write his 'true' history. López de Gómara's work is an eloquent account of both Hernán Cortés and the Conquest for which he is remembered. I have used the edition published as *Conquista de México: Segunda Parte de la Crónica General de las Indias* (Mexico: Imprenta de I. Escalante, 1870). A fine English translation by LESLEY BYRD SIMPSON entitled *Cortés, The Life of the Conqueror by his Secretary, Francisco López de Gómara* (Berkeley: University of California Press, 1966) is also available.

Bibliography

The letters and documents of Hernán Cortés collected by MARIO HERNÁNDEZ SANCHEZ BARBA and published as *Cartas y Documentos de Hernán Cortés* (Mexico: Editorial Porrua, 1963) have been immensely helpful as have *Documentos Ineditos Relativos a Hernán Cortés y su Familia* (Mexico: Talleres Graficos de la Nacion, 1935). A magnificent translation of the famous five letters Cortés wrote to Carlos V has been prepared and annotated by ANTHONY PAGDEN beneath the title *Letters from Mexico* (New Haven, Conn: Yale University Press, 1986).

The early separation of Martín Cortés from his mother is described in *Doña Marina, la Dama de la Conquista* by FEDERICO GÓMEZ DE OROZCO (Mexico: Ediciones Xochitl, 1942).

For an understanding of the world Martín Cortés entered as a six-year-old, my favorite sources proved to be *Carolus: Charles Quint 1500–1558*, edited by HANS DEVISSCHER (Ghent: Snoek-Ducaju & Zoon, 1999); *The Mediterranean and the Mediterranean World in the Age of Phillip II* (London: Collins, 1972) by the incomparable FERNAND BRAUDEL, *The Chivalrous Society* by GEORGES DUBY (London: Edward Arnold, 1977), *Knights at Court: Courtliness, Chivalry and Courtesy from Ottonian Germany to the Italian Renaissance* by ALDO SCAGLIONE (Berkeley: University of California Press, 1991), *Philip of Spain* by HENRY KAMEN (New

Haven, Conn: Yale University Press, 1997) and *The Medici Popes (Leo X and Clement VII)* by HERBERT M. VAUGHAN (New York: G.P. Putnam's Sons, 1908). Also *Extremadura y América* by MARIANO CUESTA DOMINGO (Madrid: Editorial MAPFRE, 1992), and *Centuries of Childhood: a Social History of Family Life* by PHILIPPE ARIES (New York: Random House, 1962).

Two wonderful works about costume were immensely helpful: *Authentic Everyday Dress of the Renaissance: All 154 Plates from the Trachtenbuch of Christoph Weiditz* (New York: Dover Publications); an English-language facsimile of *Trachtenbuch des Christoph Weiditz von seinen Reisen nach Spanien (1529) und den Niederlanden (1531/32)*; also *Hispanic Costume, 1480–1530* by RUTH MATILDA ANDERSON (New York: Hispanic Society of America, 1979), with its detailed plates and insightful text.

Several famous studies offer a sense of the complexities of life in Mexico in the aftermath of Conquest: GEORGE KUBLER's *Mexican Colonial Architecture of the Sixteenth Century* (Westport, Conn: Greenwood Press, 1972); CHARLES GIBSON's *The Aztecs Under Spanish Rule: A History of the Indians of the Valley of Mexico 1519–1810* (Stanford, Calif: Stanford University Press, 1964); JAMES LOCKHART's *The Nahuas after the Conquest: A Social and Cultural History of the Indians of Central Mexico, Sixteenth through*

Bibliography

Eighteenth Centuries (Stanford, Calif: Stanford University Press, 1992); and *Sir Thomas More in New Spain: A Utopian Adventure of the Renaissance* by SILVIO ZAVALA (London: Hispanic and Luso-Brazilian Councils, 1955).

On the subject of slavery and human rights in sixteenth-century Mexico two of SILVO ZAVALA's other studies have also been illuminating: *The Defence of Human Rights in Latin America* (Belgium: UNESCO, 1964) and *Los Esclavos Indios en Nueva España,* (Edición del Colegio Nacional Luis Gonzalez Obregon num. 23 Mexico 1 D.F. MCMLXVII). LEWIS HANKE's works on this important subject have also helped, especially *All Mankind is One: A Study of the Disputation between Bartolomé de Las Casas and Juan Gines de Sepulveda in 1550 on the Intellectual and Religious Capacity of the American Indians* (DeKalb: Northern Illinois University Press, 1974). The voice of BARTOLOMÉ DE LAS CASAS himself can be heard through his *Brevísima Relación de la Destrucción de las Indias,* Ed. Consuelo Varela (Madrid: Editorial Castalia, 1999).

G. MICHAEL RILEY's study, *Fernando Cortés and the Marquesado in Morelos 1522–1547: A Case Study of Socioeconomic Development in Sixteenth-Century Mexico* (Albuquerque: University of New Mexico Press, 1973) has been invaluable, as has *The Sugar*

Hacienda of the Marquéses del Valle by WARD BARRETT (Minneapolis: University of Minnesota Press, 1970), with its detailed analysis of the marquesado's economic structure.

JUAN SUÁREZ DE PERALTA left a personal account of the conspiracy trials he witnessed in Mexico City in 1566–68. I used the 1949 edition of his work published by Mexico's Secretaria de Educación Pública beneath the title *Tratado de Descubrimiento de Las Indias (Noticias Históricas de Nueva España)*. The original transcripts of the trial of Martín Cortés and his brother the second Marqués del Valle are held in the Harkness Collection of the Library of Congress, Washington D.C., and if the events of 11 September 2001, had not occurred as I was setting out for the USA and Mexico I would have gone there to read them. Instead I used the transcripts prepared by MANUEL OROZCO Y BERRA and published in his *Noticia Histórica de la Conjuración del Marqués del Valle: Años de 1565–1568*. Ed. Del Universal (Mexico: Tip de R. Rafael, 1853).

The only English language account of the conspiracy trials of 1566–68 that I know of is a painstaking and perceptive doctoral dissertation entitled T*he Avila-Cortés Conspiracy: Creole Aspirations and Royal Interests*, prepared by VICTORIA A. VINCENT, and presented to the Faculty of the Graduate College of the University of Nebraska in May 1993. The dissertation is held in the University of Nebraska library, Lincoln, Nebraska.

Bibliography

ELAINE SCARRY's *The Body in Pain: The Making and Unmaking of the World* (New York: Oxford University Press, 1985) is a moving study of torture and its effect on the human body, and soul. *Torture and the Law of Proof: Europe and England in the Ancien Regime* by JOHN H. LANGBEIN (Chicago and London: University of Chicago Press, 1977) offers a valuable contextual explanation of the role of torture in sixteenth-century Europe.

For an understanding of Islamic Spain and the Morisco Rebellion I turned to *Muslim Spain and Portugal: a Political History of Al-Andaluz* by HUGH KENNEDY (London, New York: Longman, 1996), *Guerra de Granada Hecha por El Rey Don Felipe II* by DIEGO HURTADO DE MENDOZA, *Islam and the West: The Moriscos, A Cultural and Social History* by ANWAR G. CHEJNE (Albany: State University of New York Press, 1980) and *The Forgotten Frontier: A History of the Sixteenth-Century Ibero-African Frontier,* by ANDREW HESS (Chicago and London: University of Chicago Press, 1978).

The writings of DOMINGO DE SAN ANTÓN MUÑÓN CHIMALPAHIN QUAUHTLEHUANITZIN, who translated López de Gómara's work into Náhuatl, have recently been rendered into English by ARTHUR O. ANDERSON and SUSAN SCHROEDER. Their translation is entitled *Codex Chimalpahin* (Norman and London: University of

Oklahoma Press, 1997). Through it the voice of this seventeenth-century mestizo intellectual shines again.

Researching and writing this book has allowed me to revisit WILLIAM PRESCOTT's *Conquest of Mexico* (New York: J.M. Dent and Sons, 1909) and SALVADOR DE MADARIAGA's *Hernán Cortés, Conqueror of Mexico* (Coral Gables, Florida: University of Miami Press, 1942). Both were best-sellers in their own time, and both still make wonderful reading. CARLOS FUENTES' tale of the brothers called Martín Cortés can be found in *The Orange Tree*, translated from Spanish by Alfred MacAdam (New York: Farrar, Straus and Giroux, 1994).

Index

Index

Falces, Marqués de: arrives, 189; defuses tension in Mexico City, 190; to Spain, 221

Felipe II: as prince, 46, 50; assumes Spanish throne, 111; death of mother, Isabel, 76; death of wife and son, 225; Morisco Rebellion, 234; recalls judges, 221

Ferdinand of Aragon, 39, 52

Fuentes, Carlos: *The Orange Tree*, 240–1

Galindo, Alejandro: *The Trial of Martín Cortés*, 239–40

Gandia, Duke of, 76–7

Garcia Lorca, Federico, 115, 236

Gómez de Orozco, Federico, 6, 10, 243–5, 247

Gómez de Vitoria: executed, 210; last confession, 208–10; tortured, 205

Granada, War of, *see* Morisco Rebellion

Gutierrez, Pedro Aculan Moctezuma, 62

Isabel, Empress, wife of Carlos V: arrives in Spain, 59; death, 75–7

Isabella of Castille, 39, 52,

Islamic Spain, 18–19, 234–6

La Rábida, Santa Maria de, 21–3

Las Casas, Bartolomé de, 38, 40, 95, 92, 94, 227

López de Gómara, Francisco, 28–30, 33, 82–3, 105, 227–8

Machiavelli, Niccolò, 31, 66

Maldonado, Bernardino: executed, 215; tortured, 205

Malinche: as slave, 124; costume, 12; death, 68; gives birth to Martín Cortés, 3–6; in testimony of Martín Cortés, 216; poem about, 161; separated from him, 6–12

Marina, *see* Malinche

marquesado, 148–53: confiscated, 232

Matlequeni, Benito: Spain, 63

Medellín, 26–30

Medici, Alessandro de: illegitimate son of Clemente VII, 65

Medici, Giulio de, *see* Clemente VII

Mendoça, Luis López de, *see* Quesada, Luis de

mestizos in New Spain, 126, 135–6

Mexico-Tenochtitlán, 128–34

Moctezuma, Aztec emperor, 13, 14, 62, 52, 130

Moctezuma, Isabel: daughter by Cortés, 53; estates in Mexico City, 52

Moctezuma, Leonor, 14, 53, 89

Moctezuma, Martín Cortés, *see* Cortés Nezahualzolotl, Martín

Molina, Chico de: tortured, 205

Monroy, Alonso de, 30, 233

Montesinos, Antonio de: condemns slavery, 92

Morisco Rebellion, 234–8: exile of Moriscos, 237–8

Muñoz, Alonso: arrives in Mexico, 193; exiles Martín Cortés, 212–14; leaves for Spain, 221; sentences Martín Cortés to torture, 195

New Laws, Nuevas Leyes, 156

New Spain, definition, 125

271